THE *REVISED* H. P. LOVECRAFT BIBLIOGRAPHY

By MARK OWINGS   With JACK L. CHALKER

THE *REVISED*
H. P. LOVECRAFT
BIBLIOGRAPHY

Books by MARK OWINGS

THE NECRONOMICON: A STUDY

THE ELECTRIC BIBLIOGRAPH

ROBERT A. HEINLEIN: A BIBLIOGRAPHY

CATALOGUE OF THE GRILL COLLECTION

Books by JACK L. CHALKER

THE NEW H. P. LOVECRAFT BIBLIOGRAPHY

IN MEMORIAM: CLARK ASHTON SMITH (editor)

MIRAGE ON LOVECRAFT (editor)

Books by JACK L. CHALKER and MARK OWINGS

INDEX TO THE SCIENCE FANTASY PUBLISHERS

THE *REVISED*

H. P. LOVECRAFT

BIBLIOGRAPHY

By Mark Owings

With Jack L. Chalker

THE MIRAGE PRESS, Ltd.

P. O. Box 7687, Baltimore, Maryland 21207 U. S. A.

1973

Library of Congress catalogue number: 72-85408

ISBN-0-88358-010-1

Using This

Bibliography

BIBLIOGRAPHIES NEED, of course, to be updated from time to time, and this is the first total revision of the basic Lovecraft bibliography in almost eight years. Users of earlier forms will note the vastly altered format and the elimination of some peripheral sections. If you think something—whether an entry or a category—should be in here, by all means let us know. The bibliography has been and will continue to be periodically updated every few years and is a continuing project.

As for the format, it has been changed to facilitate usage. The poems and essays are, of course, alphabetical, as in the past—but now many contain cross-references to other books in which they also appeared. In the interest of simplicity, these have been grouped by codes. Since there are four books called THE DUNWICH HORROR or variants of the same, these have been numbered one through four and appear in boldface, e. g., **The Dunwich Horror 2**. Look for them in the "Collections" section in order of the numbers.

There might be some confusion when attempting to locate a novel or story published independently of a collection. Such an example is DREAM-QUEST OF UNKNOWN KADATH, Shroud edition, which is the novel only and not a collection. As such, it is listed under Part III, "Fiction," as with the short stories. When in doubt, look under "Fiction" first; it will give the independent novels, and will also show by cross-reference in what collections the novels appeared.

In as many cases as possible the bibliography this time was recompiled by searching out the actual items. Only when those items were totally unlocatable were previous bibliographies—indeed, even prior editions of this one—used, so this is definitely the most correct and authoritative bibliography of Lovecraft done to date. In 90% of the cases, we have seen and examined the actual items herein—causing some surprises. Note, for example, what happened to "Herbert West: Reanimator" when we looked in copies of *Home Brew* and discovered it to be titled very differently.

Additions and corrections are urged, nonetheless, for no bibliography is ever complete.

Thanks must go to David Williams, Ken Scher, Albert Galpin, Kalju Kirde, G. Ken Chapman, Don Tuck, and legions of others too numerous to mention for aid and information.

Mark Owings
Jack L. Chalker

Preface

THIS REPRESENTS an updating of Jack Chalker's 1965 Lovecraft bibliography, which was an updating of Chalker's 1961 booklet, which was in turn based on the earlier efforts of George Wetzel and Robert Briney . . . which ultimately goes back to *Howard Phillips Lovecraft* (1890-1937): *A Tentative Bibliography*, compiled by Francis Towner Laney and William H. Evans (*Acolyte*, FAPA Publications: Los Angeles, 1943, wpps 12). Since error could well have crept in anywhere along that line, additions and corrections would, of course, be appreciated.

This is the first time since George Wetzel's 1949 researches in the Free Library of Philadelphia that any real research has been done into Lovecraft's amateur press work, and the amount of it turned up from a small amount of ferreting makes one feel that little more than the elbow has been seen. The next edition should prove more interesting.

I would like to thank Jack Chalker and James K. Weston for assistance at different points, and most especially Irving Binkin of Binkin's Book Centre for allowing me to go through the Philip Jack Grill collection of Lovecraft material.

Mark Owings

Contents

THE *REVISED*
H. P. LOVECRAFT
BIBLIOGRAPHY

CHAPTER 1

Essays

Aᴌᴌ ᴏғ the periodicals herein mentioned are amateur press efforts, excepting only: *Arkham Sampler*, *Asherville Gazette-News*, *De Halve Maen*, *Providence Journal*, *Weird Tales*, and probably *Boy's Herald*. Chalker (1962) says there is much more early newspaper work. I would add that there is certainly much more amateur press work, some doubtless worth reprinting.

Aʟʟᴏᴡᴀʙʟᴇ Rʜʏᴍᴇ, Tʜᴇ: *The Conservative*, October, 1915.

Aᴍᴀᴛᴇᴜʀ Cʀɪᴛɪᴄɪsᴍ: in Lovecraft Collectors' Library (hereafter referred to as "LCL"), Vol. V (q. v.).

Aᴍᴀᴛᴇᴜʀ Jᴏᴜʀɴᴀʟɪsᴍ–Iᴛs Pᴏssɪʙʟᴇ Nᴇᴇᴅs ᴀɴᴅ Bᴇᴛᴛᴇʀᴍᴇɴᴛ: in The Dark Brotherhood (q. v.).

Aᴍᴀᴛᴇᴜʀ Sᴛᴀɴᴅᴀʀᴅs: *The Conservative*, January 1917.

Aᴍᴇʀɪᴄᴀɴɪsᴍ: *The United Amateur*, July 1919.

Aɴɢʟᴏ-Sᴀxᴏɴᴅᴏᴍ: in LCL, Vol. II (q. v.).

Aᴛ ᴛʜᴇ Rᴏᴏᴛ: *The United Amateur*, July 1918; in Something About Cats (q. v.).

Aᴜᴛᴏʙɪᴏɢʀᴀᴘʜʏ–Sᴏᴍᴇ Nᴏᴛᴇs ᴏɴ ᴀ Nᴏɴᴇɴᴛɪᴛʏ: *Boy's Herald*, October 1941; included in Mirage on Lovecraft, ed. Jack L. Chalker (Anthem Press: Baltimore, 1965, wpps VI n 46, $2.50); in Beyond the Wall of Sleep (q. v.); as a booklet–Arkham House: Sauk City, 1963, wpps 17, $1.00.

Bɪᴏɢʀᴀᴘʜɪᴄ ᴀɴᴅ Cʀɪᴛɪᴄᴀʟ Pʀᴇғᴀᴄᴇ: included in The Poetical Works of Jonathan Hoag (Privately printed: N. Y., 1923, pp 72).

Bᴏʟsʜᴇᴠɪsᴍ: *The Conservative*, July 1919.

Bʀɪᴇғ Aᴜᴛᴏʙɪᴏɢʀᴀᴘʜʏ ᴏғ ᴀɴ Iɴᴄᴏɴsᴇǫᴜᴇɴᴛɪᴀʟ Sᴄʀɪʙʙʟᴇʀ, Tʜᴇ: *The Silver Clarion*, April 1919; in LCL, Vol. II (q. v.).

Bʀᴜᴍᴀʟɪᴀ: *The Tryout*, December 1916.

Bʏ Pᴏsᴛ ғʀᴏᴍ Pʀᴏᴠɪᴅᴇɴᴄᴇ (letters): *The Californian*, Summer 1937.

Cᴀsᴇ ғᴏʀ Cʟᴀssɪᴄɪsᴍ, Tʜᴇ: *The United Co-operative*, June 1919.

Cᴀᴛs Vᴇʀsᴜs Dᴏɢs: *Leaves* I, Summer 1937; in Something About Cats (q. v.) *as* Something About Cats.

Cɪɢᴀʀᴇᴛᴛᴇ Cʜᴀʀᴀᴄᴛᴇʀɪᴢᴀᴛɪᴏɴ: *Fantasy Magazine*, June 1934.

Cʟᴜsᴛᴇʀs ᴀɴᴅ Nᴇʙᴜʟᴀᴇ:*see* Mysteries of the Heavens.

Cᴏᴍᴇᴛs ᴀɴᴅ Mᴇᴛᴇᴏʀs: *see* Mysteries of the Heavens.

Cᴏᴍᴇᴛs ᴀɴᴅ Mᴇᴛᴇᴏʀs II: *see* Mysteries of the Heavens.

Cᴏᴍᴍᴇɴᴛ: *The Silver Clarion*, June 1918.

Cᴏᴍᴍᴏɴᴘʟᴀᴄᴇ Bᴏᴏᴋ, Tʜᴇ: *see* Notes and Commonplace Book . . . .

Cᴏɴᴄᴇʀɴɪɴɢ "Pᴇʀsɪᴀ–Iɴ Eᴜʀᴏᴘᴇ": *The Tryout*, January 1917; in LCL, Vol. V (q. v.).

Cᴏɴғᴇssɪᴏɴ ᴏғ Uɴғᴀɪᴛʜ, A: *The Liberal*, February 1922; in LCL, Vol. I (q. v.).

Cᴏɴsᴇʀᴠᴀᴛɪᴠᴇ ᴀɴᴅ Hɪs Cʀɪᴛɪᴄs, Tʜᴇ: *The Conservative*, October 1915.

Cᴏɴsᴛᴇʟʟᴀᴛɪᴏɴs, Tʜᴇ: *see* Mysteries . . . .

CONVENTION, THE: *The Tryout*, July 1930 (as by L. Theobald).

CRIME OF THE CENTURY, THE: *The Trail*, January 1916.

DEPARTMENT OF PUBLIC CRITICISM: *The United Amateur*, November 1914, April June & August 1916, March May & July 1917. This column probably had other installments.

DESCENT TO AVERNUS, A: *Bacon's Essays*, Summer 1929; in **LCL**, Vol. **II** (q. v.).

DESPISED PASTORAL, THE: *The Conservative*, July 1918; in **Something About Cats** (q. v.).

DIGNITY OF JOURNALISM, THE: *Dowdell's Bear-Cat*, July 1915.

DISCARDED DRAUGHT OF "The Shadow over Innsmouth": *The Acolyte* #6, Spring 1944; in **Something About Cats** (q. v.).

DOES VULCAN EXIST?: *Providence Journal*, 1906; included in **H. P. L.: A Memoir**, by August Derleth (Ben Abramson: N. Y., 1945, pp 122, $2.50).

DUTCH FOOTPRINTS IN NEW ENGLAND: *De Halve Maen*, Vol. IX, #1, October 18, 1933 issue.

EARTH AND ITS MOON, THE: *see* Mysteries . . . .

ECLIPSES: *see* Mysteries . . . .

EDITORIAL: *The Conservative*, October 1915.

EDITORIAL: *The Providence Amateur*, February 1916.

EDITORIAL: *The Conservative*, July 1923.

EDITORIAL COMMENT: *The United Amateur*, November 1920.

EDITORIAL EXCERPT FROM *The United Amateur*: *Interesting Items*, July 1950.

EDITOR'S NOTE (to MacManus' "The Irish and the Fairies"): *The Providence Amateur*, February 1916.

EXCERPTS FROM THE LETTERS OF H. P. LOVECRAFT: *The Acolyte* #1, Fall 1942.

FAVORITE WEIRD STORIES OF H. P. L.: *The Fantasy Fan*, October 1934.

FOR PRESIDENT—LEO FRITTER: *The Conservative*, April 1915.

FOR WHAT DOES THE UNITED STAND?: *The United Amateur*, May 1920.

408 GROVELAND STREET: *The Tryout*, July 1921; *Boy's Herald*, January 1943.

FURTHER CRITICISM OF POETRY: *The National Amateur*, (date unknown); as a pamphlet—Press of George G. Fetter Co., Louisville, Kentucky, 1932, wpps 13; also said to have been printed as a booklet by H. C. Koenig, though no definite information is available; *The National Amateur*, December 1944.

GUIDE TO CHARLESTON, S. C., A: in **Marginalia** (q. v.); a quarto pamphlet, without publisher or date, 22 pages plus 3 pages of maps, entitled "Charleston" by H. P. Lovecraft, has been sighted. This may be the reputed Koenig printing of this essay.

HAVERHILL CONVENTION, THE: *The Tryout*, July 1918.

HELENE HOFFMAN COLE—LITTERATEUR: *The United Amateur*, May 1919.

HERITAGE OR MODERNISM: COMMON SENSE IN ART FORMS: *The Californian*, Summer 1935; in **Marginalia** (q. v.).

HISTORY AND CHRONOLOGY OF THE NECRONOMICON: The Rebel Press: Oakman, Alabama, 1938, wpps 4; *Arkham Sampler*, Winter 1948; in **Beyond the Wall of Sleep** (q. v.); *Mirage* #6; included in **The Necronomicon: A Study**, ed. Mark Owings (Mirage Press: Baltimore, 1967, wpps 32, $1.95).

HOMES AND SHRINES OF POE: *The Californian*, Winter 1934; *The Acolyte* #5, Fall 1943.

IBID.: *O-Wash-Ta-Nong*, January 1938; in **Beyond The Wall of Sleep** (q. v.).

IDEALISM AND MATERIALISM—A REFLECTION: *The National Amateur*, July 1919; *Inside* #47, March 1956; in **LCL**, Vol. **I** (q. v.); in **The Shuttered Room I** (q. v.).

IN A MAJOR KEY: *The Conservative*, July 1915.

IN DEFENSE OF DAGON: *Leaves II*, 1938.

IN MEMORIAM: HENRY ST. CLAIR WHITEHEAD: *Weird Tales*, March 1933 (published anonymously).

IN MEMORIAM: ROBERT ERVIN HOWARD: *The Phantagraph*, August 1936; *Fantasy Magazine*, August 1936; included in **Skullface & Others**, by Robert E. Howard (Arkham House: Sauk City, Wisc., 1946, pp 501, $5.00).

IN THE EDITOR'S STUDY: *The Conservative*, April & July 1915.

INFERIOR PLANETS, THE: *see* Mysteries . . . .

INTRODUCTION: included in **Collected Works of Johnathan Hoag** (Privately printed: N. Y., 1927)

JAPANESE HAKKU: *O-Wash-Ta-Nong*, January 1938.

LAST LETTER: *Arkham Collector* #4, Winter 1969.

LEAGUE, THE: *The Conservative*, July 1919.

LES MOUCHES FANTASTIQUES: in **LCL**, Vol. **V** (q. v.).

(LETTER): *Buckeye*, June 1923.

(LETTER): *Imagination*, January 1938.

(LETTER EXCERPTS): in **Dreams & Fancies** (q. v.).

(LETTER EXCERPTS): *Phantastique*, March 1938.

(LETTER EXCERPTS FROM ARGOSY): *Golden Atom*, December 1940.

(LETTER FRAGMENT): *The Olympian*, Autumn 1940.

(LETTER FRAGMENT): *Amateur Affairs*, October 1935.

LETTERS: *L'Herne* #12, April 1969.

LIFE FOR HUMANITY'S SAKE, A: *The American Amateur*, September 1920.

LIQUOR AND ITS FRIENDS: *The Conservative,* October 1915.

LITERARY COMPOSITION: *The United Amateur*, January 1920.

LITERARY REVIEW: *The Californian*, Winter 1936.

LITERATURE OF ROME, THE: *The United Amateur*, November 1918.

LOOKING BACKWARDS: *The Tryout*, February to June 1920; as a pamphlet—C. W. Smith: Haverhill, Mass., 1935, wpps 36; *The Aonian*, Autumn and Winter 1944; in LCL, Vol. V (q. v.).

LORD DUNSANY AND HIS WORK: *Eldritch Dream-Quest III*, 1963; in Marginalia (q. v.).

LOVECRAFT AS AN ILLUSTRATOR: *The Acolyte #4*, Summer 1943. Letter excerpt with printing of some Lovecraft drawings.

LOVECRAFT ON LOVE: *Arkham Collector #8*, Winter 1971. (Letter extract).

LOVECRAFT ON POETRY WRITING: *Boy's Herald*, October 1941.

LOVECRAFTIANA—EXTRACTS FROM LETTERS TO G. W. MACAULEY: *O-Wash-Ta-Nong*, Spring 1938.

MAGNIFYING POWER: *see* Mysteries . . . .

MAP OF ARKHAM: *The Acolyte #1*, Fall 1942. (A map, not an essay).

MARS AND THE ASTEROIDS: *see* Mysteries . . . .

MATERIALIST TODAY, THE: *Driftwind*, October 1926; as a pamphlet that same year (publisher unknown); in Something About Cats (q. v.).

MERLINUS REDIVIVUS: *The Conservative*, July 1918; in Something About Cats (q. v.).

METRICAL REGULARITY: *The Conservative*, July 1915.

MORE CHAIN LIGHTNING: *The United Official Quarterly*, December 1915.

MRS. MINSTER—ESTIMATES AND RECOLLECTIONS: *The Californian*, Spring 1938.

MORRIS FACTION, THE: *The Conservative*, April 1919.

MYSTERIES OF THE HEAVENS: A series of articles in the *Asherville Gazette-News*, with the following subtitles and dates:

 THE SKY AND ITS CONTENTS: February 16, 1915.

 THE SOLAR SYSTEM: February 20, 1915.

 THE SUN: February 23, 1915.

 THE INFERIOR PLANETS: February 27, 1915.

 ECLIPSES: March 2, 1915.

 THE EARTH AND ITS MOON: March 6, 1915.

 MARS AND THE ASTEROIDS: March 9, 1915.

 COMETS AND METEORS: March 13, 1915.

 THE OUTER PLANETS: March 16, 1915.

 THE STARS: March 20, 1915.

 THE STARS II: March 23, 1915.

 THE RINGS OF SATURN: March 27, 1915.

 COMETS AND METEORS II: March 30, 1915.

 CLUSTERS AND NEBULAE: April 3, 1915.

 THE CONSTELLATIONS: April 27, 1915.

 THE SUMMER STARS: May 1, 1915.

 TELESCOPES AND OBSERVATIONS: May 11, 1915.

 MAGNIFYING POWER: May 17, 1915.

The series may have continued beyond this point. Also, there are two obvious gaps in the dating, and that last entry doesn't fit the pattern.

NIETSCHEISM AND REALISM: *The Rainbow #1*, October 1921; in LCL., Vol. I (q. v.).

NOTES AND COMMONPLACE BOOK EMPLOYED BY THE LATE H. P. LOVECRAFT, INCLUDING HIS SUGGESTIONS FOR STORY WRITING, ANALYSIS OF THE WEIRD STORY, AND LIST OF CERTAIN BASIC UNDERLYING HORRORS, ETC., DESIGNED TO STIMULATE THE IMAGINATION—Futile Press: Lakeport, Calif., 1938, wpps 45, 75 copies printed but about half remained unbound. Edited by Robert H. Barlow; in Beyond the Wall of Sleep (q. v.) *as* The Commonplace Book; in The Shuttered Room (q.v.) *as* The Commonplace Book.

NOTES FOR ''At the Mountains of Madness'': in Something About Cats (q. v.).

NOTES FOR ''The Round Tower'': *Golden Atom*, Winter 1943.

NOTES FOR ''The Shadow Out of Time'': in Something About Cats (q. v.).

NOTES FOR ''The Shadow Over Innsmouth'': in Something About Cats (q. v.).

NOTES ON THE WRITING OF WEIRD FICTION: *The Amateur Correspondent*, May-June 1937; *Supermundane Stories*, Spring 1938; included in Mirage on Lovecraft, ed. Jack L. Chalker (Anthem Press: Baltimore, 1965, wpps vi + 46, $2.50); in Marginalia (q. v.).

OBSERVATIONS OF SEVERAL PARTS OF NORTH AMERICA: in Marginalia (q. v.).

OLD ENGLAND AND THE ''Hyphen'': *The Conservative*, October 1916.

OMNIPOTENT PHILISTINE, THE: *The Oracle*, May 1924.

OUTER PLANETS, THE: *see* Mysteries . . .

POETRY AND THE ARTISTIC IDEAL: *The Acolyte #3*, Spring 1943.

POETRY OF JOHN RAVENOR BULLEN: *The United Amateur*, September 1925.

PRESIDENT'S MESSAGE: *The United Amateur*, November 1917, January 1918, July 1918; the first was reprinted in LCL, Vol. V (q. v.). Others may have appeared during Lovecraft's term of office.

PRESIDENT'S REPORT, THE: *The National Amateur*, July 1923.

PROFESSIONAL INCUBUS, THE: *The National Amateur*, March 1924; in LCL. Vol. V (q. v.).

PROPOSED AUTHOR'S UNION, THE: *The Conservative*, October 1916.

QUESTION OF THE DAY, THE: *The Conservative*, April 1915.

REMARKABLE DOCUMENT, A: *The Conservative*, July 1917.

RENAISSANCE OF MANHOOD, THE: *The Conservative*, October 1915.

REPLY TO THE LINGERER, A: *The Tryout*, June 1917; in LCL, Vol. V (q. v.).

REVIEW OF SMITH'S **Ebony and Crystal**: *L'Alouette*, January 1924.

REVOLUTIONARY MYTHOLOGY: in LCL, Vol. II (q. v.).

RINGS OF SATURN, THE: *see* Mysteries . . .

RUDIS INDIGESTAQUE MOLES: *The Conservative*, March 1923; included in H. P. L.: A Memoir, by August Derleth (Ben Abramson: N. Y., 1945, pp 122, $2.50).

SIMPLE SPELLING MANIA, THE: *The United Co-operative*, December 1918; in LCL, Vol. V (q. v.).

SINGER OF ETHEREAL MOODS AND FANCIES, A: *Memoriam*, September 1921.

SKY AND ITS CONTENTS, THE: *see* Mysteries . . .

SOLAR SYSTEM, THE: *see* Mysteries . . .

SOME BACKGROUNDS OF FAIRYLAND: in **Marginalia** (q. v.); *Mirage* #8, Summer 1966.

SOME CAUSES OF SELF-IMMOLATION: in **Marginalia** (q. v.).

SOME CURRENT MOTIVES AND PRACTICES: two mimeographed sheets dated June 4, 1936, probably published by Lovecraft himself.

SOME NOTES ON INTERPLANETARY FICTION: *The Recluse*,#1, 1927; *The Californian*, Winter 1935; *The Acolyte* #4, Summer 1943; included in **Mirage on Lovecraft**, ed. Jack L. Chalker (Anthem Press: Baltimore, 1965, wpps v + 46, $2.50); in **Marginalia** (q. v.).

SOMETHING ABOUT CATS: *see* Cats Versus Dogs.

STARS, THE: *see* Mysteries . . .

STARS II, THE: *see* Mysteries . . .

SUGGESTIONS FOR A READING GUIDE: in **The Dark Brotherhood** (q. v.); *L'Herne* #12, April 1969. (Extracted from a letter.).

SUMMER STARS, THE: *see* Mysteries . . .

SUN, THE: *see* Mysteries . . .

SUPERNATURAL HORROR IN LITERATURE: *The Recluse* #1, 1927; *The Fantasy Fan*, October 1933 through February 1935 (incomplete); in **The Outsider & Others** (q. v.); in **Dagon I** (q. v.); as a separate book—Ben Abramson: N. Y., 1945, pp 122, $2.50. All appearances after the first represent a revised version.

SYMPHONIC IDEAL, THE: in LCL, Vol. V (q. v.).

SYMPHONY AND STRESS: *The Conservative*, October 1915.

SYSTEMATIC INSTRUCTION IN THE UNITED: *Ole Miss*, December 1915.

TELESCOPES AND OBSERVATIONS: see Mysteries . . . .

TEUTON'S BATTLE SONG, THE: *The United Amateur*, February 1916.

TIME AND SPACE: *The Conservative*, July 1918; in **Something About Cats** (q. v.).

TRIP OF THEOBALD, THE: *The Tryout*, September 1927 (as by L. Theobald, Jr.); in LCL, Vol. II (q. v.).

TRUTH ABOUT MARS, THE: *The Phoenician*, Autumn 1917.

UNKNOWN CITY IN THE OCEAN, THE: *The Perspective Review*, Winter 1934.

VERMONT: *Driftwood*, March 1928; in **Something About Cats** (q. v.) *as* Vermont: A First Impression.

VERS LIBRÉ EPIDEMIC, THE: *The Conservative*, January 1917.

VIVISECTOR, THE: *The Wolverine*, June 1921 (as by Zoilus).

WEIRD WORK OF WILLIAM HOPE HODGSON, THE: *The Phantagraph*, February 1937.

WHAT BELONGS IN VERSE: *The Perspective Review*, Spring 1935; *L'Herne* #12, April 1969; in **The Dark Brotherhood** (q. v.).

WINIFRED JACKSON: *The United Amateur*, March 1921.

YOUTH OF TODAY, THE: *The Conservative,* October 1915.

CHAPTER 2

Verse

Here the only professional publication, excepting newspapers, is *Weird Tales*. And again there is undoubtedly much more amateur press work, especially under pseudonyms.

ABSENT LEADER, THE: in the chapbook In Memory of Hazel Adams (1927).

AD BRITTANOS, 1918: *The Tryout*, April 1918.

AD CRITICOS: *Golden Atom*, December 1940.

AD SCRIBAM: *The Tryout*, February 1920; included in The Poetical Works of Jonathan E. Hoag (Privately printed: N. Y., 1923, pp 72).

ALETHIA PHRIKOIDES: *see* The Poe-et's Nightmare.

ALFREDO: in The Dark Brotherhood (q.v.).

ALIENATION: *Weird Tales*, April-May 1931; in Fungi from Yuggoth (q.v.); in Beyond the Wall of Sleep (q.v.); in Collected Poems (q.v.); included in Dark of the Moon, ed. August Derleth (Arkham House: Sauk City, 1947, pp xvi + 418, $3.00).

AMBITION: *The United Co-operative*, December 1918; in LCL, Vol. III (q.v.).

AMERICAN TO THE BRITISH FLAG, AN: *Little Budget*, December 1917.

AMERICAN TO MOTHER ENGLAND, AN: *Dowell's Bear-Cat*, November 1916.

AMISSA MINERVA: *The Toledo Amateur*, May 1919.

ANCIENT TRACK, THE: *Weird Tales*, March 1930; included in Dark of the Moon, ed. August Derleth (Arkham House: Sauk City, 1947, pp xvi + 418, $3.00); in Beyond the Wall of Sleep (q.v.); in Collected Poems (q.v.).

ANTARKTOS: *Weird Tales*, November 1930; included in Dark of the Moon, ed. August Derleth (Arkham House: Sauk City, 1947, pp xvi + 418, $3.00); in

Fungi from Yuggoth (q.v.); in Beyond the Wall of Sleep (q.v.); in Collected Poems (q.v.).

APRIL: *The Tryout*, March 1918.

ASTROPHOBOS: *The United Amateur*, January 1918; *Phantasmagoria*, March 1937; *Golden Atom*, March 1940; in H. P. L. (q.v.); in Beyond the Wall of Sleep (q.v.); in Collected Poems (q.v.).

AUGUST: *The Tryout*, August 1918; *The Californian*, Summer 1937; in Something About Cats (q.v.); in Collected Poems (q.v.).

AUTUMN: *The Tryout*, November 1917; in LCL, Vol. III (q.v.).

AVE ATQUE VALE: *The Tryout*, December 1927; in LCL, Vol. IV (q.v.).

AZATHOTH: *Weird Tales*, January 1931; included in Dark of the Moon, ed. August Derleth (Arkham House: Sauk City, 1947, pp xvi + 418, $3.00); in Fungi from Yuggoth (q.v.); in Beyond the Wall of Sleep (q.v.); in Collected Poems (q.v.).

BACKGROUND: evidently first printed in Fungi from Yuggoth (q.v.); included in Dark of the Moon, ed. August Derleth (Arkham House: Sauk City, 1947, pp xvi + 418, $3.00); in Beyond the Wall of Sleep (q.v.); in Collected Poems (q.v.).

BEAUTIES OF PEACE, THE: *Providence News*, June 17, 1916.

BELLS: *The Tryout*, December 1919; in LCL, Vol. III (q.v.); in The Dark Brotherhood (q.v.).

BELLS, THE: *Weird Tales*, December 1930; included in **Dark of the Moon**, ed. August Derleth (Arkham House: Sauk City, 1947, pp xvi + 418, $3.00); in **Fungi from Yuggoth** (q. v.); in **Beyond the Wall of Sleep** (q. v.); in **Collected Poems** (q. v.).

BOOK, THE: *The Fantasy Fan*, October 1934; *Driftwind*, April 1937; included in **Dark of the Moon**, ed. August Derleth (Arkham House: Sauk City, 1947, pp xvi + 418, $3.00); in **Fungi from Yuggoth** (q. v.); in **Collected Poems** (q. v.); in **Beyond the Wall of Sleep** (q. v.).

BOOKSTALL, THE: *The United Official Quarterly*, January 1916; in **LCL, Vol. III** (q. v.).

BRICK ROW: in **Beyond the Wall of Sleep** (q. v.); in **Collected Poems** (q. v.).

BRIDE OF THE SEA, THE: *The Providence Amateur*, February 1916 (as by L. Theobald); *O-Wash-Ta-Nong*, December 1937; *Phantagraph*, August 1941.

BRITTANIA VICTURA: *Inspiration*, April 1917; *Little Budget*, May 1917.

BROTHERHOOD: *The Tryout*, December 1916 (as by L. Theobald, Jr.).

BRUMALIA: *The Tryout*, December 1916.

CANAL, THE: *Driftwind*, March 1932; *Weird Tales*, January 1938; included in **Dark of the Moon**, ed. August Derleth (Arkham House: Sauk City, 1947; pp xvi + 418, $3.00); in **Fungi from Yuggoth** (q. v.); in **Beyond the Wall of Sleep** (q. v.); in **Collected Poems** (q. v.).

CHLORIS AND DAMON: *The Tryout*, June 1923 (as by Edward Softly).

CHRISTMAS: *The Tryout*, November 1920 (as by Edward Softly).

CHRISTMAS GREETINGS TO MRS. PHILLIPS GAMWELL, 1925: in **Beyond the Wall of Sleep** (q. v.); in **Collected Poems** (q. v.).

CINDY—SCRUB LADY IN A STATE STREET SKYSCRAPER: *The Tryout*, June 1920; in **LCL, Vol. IV** (q. v.); in **The Dark Brotherhood** (q. v.).

CITY, THE: *The Vagrant*, October 1919 (as by Ward Phillips); *Weird Tales*, July 1950; in **Beyond the Wall of Sleep** (q. v.); in **Collected Poems** (q. v.).

CLOUDS: *The Tryout*, July 1919; *Stars*, June 1940; *Spaceways*, February 1939; *Fantasy Commentator*, Spring 1948, in **LCL, Vol. IV** (q. v.); in **The Dark Brotherhood** (q. v.).

COMMENT: *The Tryout*, July 1920.

CONTENT: *The United Amateur*, June 1915.

CONTINUITY: *Causerie*, February 1936; *The Acolyte* #4, Summer 1943; *Weird Tales*, March 1947; in **Beyond the Wall of Sleep** (q. v.); in **Collected Poems** (q. v.); included in **Dark of the Moon**, ed. August Derleth (Arkham House: Sauk City, 1947, pp xvi + 418, $3.00); included in **Unseen Wings**, ed. Stanton A. Coblentz (Beechhurst Press: N. Y., 1949, pp 282, $4.50); included in **The Pulps**, ed. Tony Goodstone (Chelsea House: N. Y., 1970, pp 239, $15.00).

COURTYARD, THE: *Weird Tales*, September 1930; included in **Dark of the Moon**, ed. August Derleth (Arkham House: Sauk City, 1947, pp xvi + 418, $3.00); in **Fungi from Yuggoth** (q. v.); in **Beyond the Wall of Sleep** (q. v.); in **Collected Poems** (q. v.).

CRIME OF CRIMES, THE: *Interesting Items*, July 1915.

CUP BEARER, THE: *Asmodeus*, Fall 1915.

DAMON—A MONODY: *The United Amateur*, May 1919 (as by Theobaldus Senectissimus, Esq.).

DAMON AND DELIA: *The Tryout*, August 1918 (as by Edward Softly).

DEAD BOOKWORM, THE: *The United Amateur*, September 1919 (as by John J. Jones); in **LCL, Vol. IV** (q. v.).

DEATH: *The Californian*, Summer 1937; in **Something About Cats** (q. v.); in **Collected Poems** (q. v.).

DESPAIR: *Pine Cones*, December 1919 (as by Ward Phillips); in **Beyond the Wall of Sleep** (q. v.); in **Collected Poems** (q. v.).

DREAM: *The Tryout*, September 1920 (as by Edward Softly); in **LCL, Vol. IV** (q. v.).

DRINKING SONG FROM "The Tomb": in **Collected Poems** (q. v.). Only separate publication.

DWELLER, THE: *Weird Tales*, March 1940; included in **Dark of the Moon**, ed. August Derleth (Arkham House: Sauk City, 1947, pp xvi + 418, $3.00); included in **The Macabre Reader**, ed. Donald A. Wollheim (Ace: N. Y., D-353, 1959, wpps 223, 35¢) (Digit: London D-362, 1960, wpps 188, 2s); in **H. P. L.** (q. v.); in **Fungi from Yuggoth** (q. v.); in **Beyond the Wall of Sleep** (q. v.); in **Collected Poems** (q. v.).

EARTH AND SKY: *Little Budget*, July 1917; *Pine Cones*, December 1918; in **LCL, Vol. IV** (q. v.).

EDITH MINITER: in the chapbook *In Memory of Edith Miniter*.

EIDOLON, THE: *The Tryout*, October 1918 (as by Ward Phillips); in **Beyond the Wall of Sleep** (q. v.); in **Collected Poems** (q. v.).

ELDER PHAROS, THE: *Weird Tales*, February-March 1931; included in Dark of the Moon, ed. August Derleth (Arkham House: Sauk City, 1947, pp xvi + 418, $3.00); in Fungi from Yuggoth (q. v.); in Beyond the Wall of Sleep (q. v.); in Collected Poems (q. v.).

ELEGY ON PHILLIPS GAMWELL, ESQ,: *The Providence News*, January 5, 1917.

ELEGY ON REV. F. C. CLARK: *The Providence News*, April 29, 1915.

EPILOGUE TO "The Bride of the Sea": *O-Wash-Ta-Nong*, December 1937; *Phantagraph*, August 1941.

EPILOGUE TO "A Summer Sunset and Evening": *O-Wash-Ta-Nong*, December 1937.

EPILOGUE TO "The Introduction": *O-Wash-Ta-Nong*, December 1937.

EPILOGUE TO "The Peace Advocate": *O-Wash-Ta-Nong*, December 1937.

EPISTLE TO RHEINHART KLEINER, AN: *The United Amateur*, June 1916.

EVENING STAR: *Weird Tales*, May 1944; included in Dark of the Moon, ed. August Derleth (Arkham House: Sauk City, 1947, pp xvi + 418, $3.00); in Beyond the Wall of Sleep (q. v.); in Collected Poems (q. v.).

EXPECTANCY: in Fungi from Yuggoth (q. v.); included in Dark of the Moon, ed. August Derleth (Arkham House: Sauk City, 1947, pp xvi + 418, $3.00); in Beyond the Wall of Sleep (q. v.); in Collected Poems (q. v.).

EX-POET'S REPLY: *Epegephi*, July 1920 (as by L. Theobald, Jr.).

FACT AND FANCY: *The Tryout*, February 1917; in LCL, Vol. IV (q. v.).

FAMILIARS, The: *Driftwind*, July 1930; *Weird Tales*, January 1947; included in Dark of the Moon, ed. August Derleth (Arkham House: Sauk City, 1947, pp xvi + 418, $3.00); in Fungi from Yuggoth (q. v.); in Beyond the Wall of Sleep (q. v.); in Collected Poems (q. v.).

FEAST, THE: *Hub Club Quill*, May 1923.

FRAGMENT ON WHITMAN: *The Conservative*, July 1915.

FUTURISTIC ART: *The Conservative*, January 1917.

GARDEN, A: *The Vagrant*, Spring 1927; in LCL, Vol. IV (q. v.).

GARDENS OF YIN, THE: *Driftwind*, March 1932; *Weird Tales*, August 1939; included in H. P. L., A Memoir, by August Derleth (Ben Abramson: N. Y., 1945, pp 122, $2.50); included in Dark of the Moon, ed. August Derleth (Arkham House: Sauk

City, 1947, pp xvi + 418, $3.00); included in The Pulps, ed. Tony Goodstone (Chelsea House: N. Y., 1970, pp 239, $15.00); in Fungi from Yuggoth (q. v.); in Beyond the Wall of Sleep (q. v.); in Collected Poems (q. v.).

GEMS FROM "In a Minor Key": *The Conservative*, July 1915.

GEORGE WILLARD KIRK: *The National Amateur*, May 1927.

GERMANIA—1918: *The Tryout*, November 1918.

GRACE: *The Conservative*, July 1918 (as by Ward Phillips); in LCL, Vol. IV (q. v.).

HALLOWE'EN IN A SUBURB: *The National Amateur*, March 1926 as In a Suburb; *Phantagraph*, June 1937; *Weird Tales*, September 1952; in Beyond the Wall of Sleep (q. v.); in Collected Poems (q. v.).

HARBOUR WHISTLES: *The Silver Fern*, May 1930; *Phantagraph*, November 1936; *Weird Tales*, May 1939; included in Dark of the Moon, ed. August Derleth (Arkham House: Sauk City, 1947, pp xvi + 418, $3.00); included in Operation Phantasy, ed. Donald A. Wollheim (Phantagraph Press: Rego Park, N. Y., 1967, pp 59, $4.00); in H. P. L. (q. v.); in Fungi from Yuggoth (q. v.); in Beyond the Wall of Sleep (q. v.); in Collected Poems (q. v.).

HELLAS: *The United Amateur*, September 1918.

HESPERIA: *Weird Tales*, October 1930; included in Dark of the Moon, ed. August Derleth (Arkham House: Sauk City, 1947, pp xvi + 418, $3.00); in Fungi from Yuggoth (q. v.); in Beyond the Wall of Sleep (q. v.); in Collected Poems (q. v.).

HOMECOMING: *The Fantasy Fan*, January 1935; *Weird Tales*, May 1944; included in Dark of the Moon, ed. August Derleth (Arkham House: Sauk City, 1947, pp xvi + 418, $3.00); in H. P. L. (q. v.); in Fungi from Yuggoth (q. v.); in Beyond the Wall of Sleep (q. v.); in Collected Poems (q. v.).

HOUSE, THE: *The Philosopher*, December 1920 (as by Ward Phillips); *Weird Tales*, March 1948; in Something About Cats (q. v.); in Collected Poems (q. v.).

HOWLER, THE: *Driftwind*, November 1932; *Weird Tales*, July 1939; included in Dark of the Moon, ed. August Derleth (Arkham House: Sauk City 1947, pp xvi + 418, $3.00); in Fungi from Yuggoth (q. v.); in Beyond the Wall of Sleep (q. v.); in Collected Poems (q. v.).

HYLAS AND MYRRAH: *The Tryout*, May 1919 (as by Laurence Appleton); in LCL, Vol. III (q. v.).

IN A SEQUESTERED GRAVEYARD WHERE ONCE POE WALKED: *see* Where Once Poe Walked.

IN A SUBURB: *see* Hallowe'en in a Suburb.

IN MEMORIAM: *The Tryout*, March 1919 (as by Ward Phillips).

INSPIRATION: *The Conservative*, October 1916 (as by Lewis Theobald); in LCL, Vol. III (q.v.).

INTRODUCTION,THE: *O-Wash-Ta-Nong*, December 1937.

INTERUM CONJUNCTAE: *The Tryout*, May 1917; *Little Budget*, September 1917; *The Tryout*, May 1938; in LCL, Vol. III (q.v.).

JOHN OLDHAM—A DEFENSE: *The United Co-operative*, June 1919.

JUNE AFTERNOON, A: *The Tryout*, June 1918; *Vanity Fair*, September 1919.

KEY, THE: *The Fantasy Fan*, January 1935; in Fungi from Yuggoth (q.v.); in Beyond the Wall of Sleep (q.v.); in Collected Poems (q.v.).

LAETA—A LAMENT: *The Tryout*, February 1918 (as by Ames Dorrance Rowley).

LAMP, THE: *Driftwind*, March 1931; *Weird Tales*, February 1939; included in Dark of the Moon, ed. August Derleth (Arkham House: Sauk City, 1947, pp xvi + 418, $3.00); in Fungi from Yuggoth (q.v.); in Beyond the Wall of Sleep (q.v.); in Collected Poems (q.v.).

LINES FOR POET'S NIGHT: *The National Amateur*, January 1924; *Pegasus*, February 1924; in LCL, Vol. IV (q.v.) *as* Lines for the Poet's Night at the Scribbler's Club.

LINES ON GENERAL ROBERT E. LEE: *Coyote*, January 1917.

LINES ON GRADUATION FROM R. I. HOSPITAL SCHOOL OF NURSES: *The Tryout*, February 1917 (as by John T. Dunne).

LINES ON THE 25TH ANNIVERSARY OF *The Providence Evening News*: *The Tryout*, December 1917; in LCL, Vol. IV (q.v.).

LINK, THE: *The Tryout*, July 1918.

LITTLE SAM PERKINS: in Collected Poems (q.v.).

MAGAZINE POET, THE: *The United Amateur*, September 1915.

MARCH: *The United Amateur*, March 1915.

MEMORY, A: *Weird Tales*, March 1947; included in Dark of the Moon, ed. August Derleth (Arkham House: Sauk City, 1947, pp xvi + 418, $3.00); included in Unseen Wings, ed. Stanton A. Coblentz (Beechhurst Press: N. Y., 1948, pp 282, $4.50); in Fungi from Yuggoth (q.v.); in Beyond the Wall of Sleep (q.v.); in Collected Poems (q.v.).

MESSENGER, THE: *Weird Tales*, July 1938; included in Dark of the Moon, ed. August Derleth (Arkham House: Sauk City, 1947, pp xvi + 418, $3.00); in Beyond the Wall of Sleep (q.v.); in Collected Poems (q.v.).

MIRAGE: *Weird Tales*, February-March 1931; *Mirage* #5, Spring 1962; included in Dark of the Moon, ed. August Derleth (Arkham House: Sauk City, 1947, pp xvi + 418, $3.00); in Fungi from Yuggoth (q.v.); in Beyond the Wall of Sleep (q.v.); in Collected Poems (q.v.).

MISSISSIPPI AUTUMN, A: *Ole Miss*, December 1915.

MONAS—AN ODE: *The Silver Clarion*, October 1918; in LCL, Vol. III (q.v.).

MONODY ON THE LATE KING ALCOHOL: *The Tryout*, August 1919 (as by Lewis Theobald).

MOTHER EARTH: *The Tryout*, July 1919 (as by Ward Phillips); in LCL, Vol. IV (q.v.); in The Dark Brotherhood (q.v.).

MY FAVORITE CHARACTER: *The United Amateur*, July 1918; *Brooklynite*, January 1926; in Something About Cats (q.v.); in Collected Poems (q.v.).

MYRRA AND STREPHON: *The Tryout*, July 1919 (as by Lawrence Appleton).

NATHICANA: *The Vagrant*, Spring 1927 (as by Albert Frederick Willie); in LCL, Vol. IV (q.v.); in The Doom that Came to Sarnath (q.v.).

NEMESIS: *The Vagrant*, July 1918; *Weird Tales*, April 1924; in Beyond the Wall of Sleep (q.v.); in Collected Poems (q.v.). A portion of the verse precedes all printings of the story "The Haunter of the Dark." (q.v.).

NEW ENGLAND FALLEN: in Beyond the Wall of Sleep (q.v.); in Collected Poems (q.v.).

NIGHT-GAUNTS: *Phantagraph*, June 1936; *Weird Tales*, December 1939; included in Dark of the Moon, ed. August Derleth (Arkham House: Sauk City, 1947, pp xvi + 418, $3.00); included in The Macabre Reader, ed. Donald A. Wollheim (Ace: N. Y., D-353, 1959, wpps 223, 35¢) (Digit: London, D-362, 1960, wpps 188, 2s); in H. P. L. (q.v.); in Fungi from Yuggoth (q.v.); in Beyond the Wall of Sleep (q.v.); in Dreams & Fancies (q.v.); in Collected Poems (q.v.).

NIGHTMARE LAKE, THE: *The Vagrant*, December 1919; *Scienti-Snaps*, Summer 1940; in Beyond the Wall of Sleep (q.v.); in Collected Poems (q.v.).

1914: *Interesting Items*, March 1914.

PRIMAVERA: *The Brooklynite*, April 1925; *Interesting Items*, April 1950; in Beyond the Wall of Sleep (q. v.); in Collected Poems (q. v.).

PROLOGUE: *The Tryout*, July 1917; in LCL, Vol. IV (q. v.).

PROVIDENCE: *The Brooklynite*, November 1924; *The Brooklynite*, May 1927; *The Californian*, Summer 1937; in Beyond the Wall of Sleep (q. v.); in Collected Poems (q. v.).

PSYCHOPOMPOS: *The Vagrant*, October 1919; *Weird Tales*, September 1937; included in Dark of the Moon, ed. August Derleth (Arkham House: Sauk City, 1947, pp xvi + 418, $3.00); in Beyond the Wall of Sleep (q. v.); in Collected Poems (q. v.).

PURSUIT: *The Fantasy Fan*, October 1934; included in Dark of the Moon, ed. August Derleth (Arkham House: Sauk City, 1947, pp xvi + 418, $3.00); in Fungi from Yuggoth (q. v.); in Beyond the Wall of Sleep (q. v.); in Collected Poems (q. v.).

QUINSNICKET PARK: *The Badger*, June 1915.

RECAPTURE: *Weird Tales*, May 1930; *Weird Tales*, January 1946; included in Dark of the Moon, ed. August Derleth (Arkham House: Sauk City, 1947, pp xvi + 418, $3.00); in Beyond the Wall of Sleep (q. v.); in Collected Poems (q. v.).

RECOGNITION: *Driftwind*, December 1936; included in Dark of the Moon, ed. August Derleth (Arkham House: Sauk City, 1947, pp xvi + 418, $3.00); in Fungi from Yuggoth (q. v.); in Beyond the Wall of Sleep (q. v.); in Collected Poems (q. v.).

REGNAR LODBRUG'S EPICEDIUM: *Acolyte* #9, Summer 1944; in Something About Cats (q. v.); in Collected Poems (q. v.).

RESPITE: *The Conservative*, October 1916.

RETURN, THE: *The Tryout*, December 1926.

REVELATION: *The Tryout*, March 1919.

RHEINHART KLEINER, LAUREATUS: *The Conservative*, April 1916.

ROSE OF ENGLAND, THE: *The Scot*, October 1916.

RURAL SUMMER EVE, A: *The Trail*, January 1916.

RUTTED ROAD, THE: *The Tryout*, January 1917 (as by L. Theobald); *The Tryout*, March 1926; in Beyond the Wall of Sleep (q. v.); in Collected Poems (q. v.).

ST. TOAD'S: *Weird Tales*, May 1944; included in Dark of the Moon, ed. August Derleth (Arkham House: Sauk City, 1947, pp xvi + 418, $3.00); in Fungi from Yuggoth (q. v.); in Beyond the Wall of Sleep (q. v.); in Collected Poems (q. v.).

SIMPLE SPELLER'S TALE, THE: *The Conservative*, April 1915.

SINGER OF ETHEREAL MOODS AND FANCIES, A: *Memoriam*, September 1921.

SIR THOMAS TRYOUT: *The Tryout*, December 1921 (as by Ward Phillips); *The Tryout*, March 1941; in Something About Cats (q. v.); in Collected Poems (q. v.).

SIR THOMAS TRYOUT'S LAMENT FOR THE VANISHED SPIDER: *see* Tryout's Lament . . .

SMILE, THE: *Symphony*, July 1916; *Little Budget*, September 1917.

SOLSTICE: *The Tryout*, January 1925 (as by Lewis Theobald, Jr.); in LCL, Vol. IV (q. v.).

SONNET, A: *The Lovecrafter*, August 20, 1936.

SONNET ON MYSELF, A: *The Tryout*, July 1918.

SPIRIT OF SUMMER, THE: *The Conservative*, July 1918.

SPRING: *The Tryout*, April 1919.

STAR-WINDS: *Weird Tales*, September 1930; included in Dark of the Moon, ed. August Derleth (Arkham House: Sauk City, 1947, pp xvi + 418, $3.00); in Fungi from Yuggoth (q. v.); in Beyond the Wall of Sleep (q. v.); in Collected Poems (q. v.).

STATE OF POETRY, THE: *The Conservative*, October 1915.

SUMMER SUNSET AND EVENING, A: *O-Wash-Ta-Nong*, December 1937; in Beyond the Wall of Sleep (q. v.); in Collected Poems (q. v.).

SUNSET: *The Tryout*, December 1917 (as by Lewis Theobald); *The United Amateur*, May 1918; *The Californian*, Summer 1937; *The Tryout*, May 1938; in Beyond the Wall of Sleep (q. v.); in Collected Poems (q. v.).

TEMPERANCE SONG: *The Dixie Booster*, Spring 1916.

TEUTON'S BATTLE SONG: *The United Amateur*, February 1916.

THEODORE ROOSEVELT: *The United Amateur*, January 1919.

TO A DREAMER: *The Coyote*, January 1921; *Weird Tales*, November 1924; in Beyond the Wall of Sleep (q. v.); in Collected Poems (q. v.).

TO A YOUTH: *The Tryout*, February 1921; in Something About Cats (q. v.); in Collected Poems (q. v.).

TO ALAN SEEGAR: *The Tryout*, July 1918; *The United Amateur*, November 1918.

TO ALFRED GALPIN: *The Tryout*, December 1920 (as by L. Theobald).

TO AN INFANT: *The Brooklynite*, October 1925.

To CHARLIE OF THE COMICS: *The Providence Amateur*, February 1916 (as by Theobald).

To CLARK ASHTON SMITH, ESQ.: *Asmodeus* #2, Fall 1951; in Beyond the Wall of Sleep (q. v.): (*as* To Clark Ashton Smith, Esq., Upon His Phantastic Tales, Verse, Pictures, and Sculptures); in Collected Poems (q. v.): (*as* To Klarkash-Ton, Lord of Averoigne).

To DAMON: *The Tryout*, August 1923 (as by Lewis Theobald).

To EDWARD PLUNKETT: *The Tryout*, November 1919; in LCL, Vol. III (q. v.).

To ENDYMION: *The Tryout*, September 1923 (as by Lewis Theobald).

To GENERAL VILLA: *The Blarney Stone*, November-December 1914.

To GREECE—1917: *The Vagrant*, November 1917; in LCL, Vol. IV (q. v.).

To JONATHAN HOAG: *The Brooklynite*, May 1926.

To JONATHAN E. HOAG, ESQ.: *The Tryout*, November 1923; this is probably in The Poetical Works of Jonathan E. Hoag *as* To Mr. Hoag Upon His 92nd Birthday.

To JONATHAN E. HOAG ON HIS 86TH BIRTHDAY: probably originally printed in *The Tryout* in early 1917; included in The Poetical Works of Jonathan E. Hoag (Privately printed: N. Y., 1923, pp 72).

To JONATHAN HOAG UPON HIS 87TH BIRTHDAY: *The Eurus*, February 1918; included in The Poetical Works of Jonathan E. Hoag (privately printed: N. Y., 1923, pp 72).

To JONATHAN HOAG UPON HIS 96TH BIRTHDAY: *The National Amateur*, May 1927.

To KLARKASH-TON, LORD OF AVEROIGNE: *see* To Clark Ashton Smith, Esq.

To MAJ.-GEN. OMAR BUNDY, USA: *The Tryout,* January 1919.

To MEMBERS OF THE UNITED AMATEUR PRESS ASSOCIATION: *The Providence Amateur*, June 1915.

To MISS BERYL HOYT: *Justice*, February 1927.

To MR. FINLAY: *see* To Virgil Finlay.

To MR. GALPIN: *The Tryout*, December 1921 (as by Lewis Theobald).

To MR. HOAG: *Pegasus*, July 1924; *The Tryout*, March 1925 (*as* To Mr. Hoag on His 94th Birthday).

To MR. HOAG ON HIS 90TH BIRTHDAY: *The Tryout*, February 1921; included in The Poetical Works of Jonathan E. Hoag (Privately printed: N. Y., 1923, pp 72).

To MR. LOCKHART, ON HIS POETRY: *The Tryout*, March 1917; in LCL, Vol. III (q. v.).

To M. W. M.: *The United Amateur*, July 1917 (anonymous).

To MISTRESS SOPHIA SIMPLE, QUEEN OF THE CINEMA: *The United Amateur*, November 1919; in Beyond the Wall of Sleep (q. v.); in Collected Poems (q. v.).

To PAN: included in H. P. L.: A Memoir, by August Derleth (Ben Abramson: N. Y., 1945, pp 122, $2.50); in Collected Poems (q. v.).

To PHILLIS: *The Tryout*, January 1920.

To RHEINHART KLEINER: *The Tryout*, April 1923 (as by Theobald).

To SAMUEL LOVEMAN, ESQUIRE: *Dowdell's Bear-Cat*, December 1915.

To SELENE: *The Tryout*, April 1919 (as by Edward Softly).

To TEMPLETON AND MOUNT MONADNOCK: *The Vagrant*, June 1917; the 1949 Arkham House catalogue; in Something About Cats (q. v.); in Collected Poems (q. v.).

To THE AMERICAN FLAG: *The Californian*, Summer 1937; *The Rochester-American Patriot*, Summer 1942; in Something About Cats (q. v.); in Collected Poems (q. v.).

To THE EIGHTH OF NOVEMBER: *The Tryout*, November 1919 (as by Archibald Maynwaring); in LCL, Vol. III (q. v.).

To THE LATE JOHN H. FOWLER, ESQ.: *The Scot*, March 1916.

To THE PINFEATHER CLUB: *The Pinfeather*, November 1914.

To THE REV. JOSEPH T. PYKE: *The United Official Quarterly*, 1914.

To VIRGIL FINLAY: *Phantagraph*, May 1937 (*as* To Mr. Finlay); *Weird Tales*, July 1937; in Beyond the Wall of Sleep (q. v.): (*as* To Mr. Finlay, Upon His Drawing for Mr. Bloch's Tale, "The Faceless God"); in Collected Poems (q. v.).

TRYOUT'S LAMENT FOR THE VANISHED SPIDER: *The Tryout*, January 1920 (as by Edward Softly); in Something About Cats (q. v.); in Collected Poems (q. v.). Later printings as "Sir Thomas Tryout's Lament . . . .").

UNTITLED POEM ("The Ancient Garden seems Tonight . . ."): *The Olympian*, Autumn 1940.

UNTITLED POEM ("Slang is the Life of Speech . . ."): *The Conservative*, April 1915.

UNTITLED POEM: *The Tryout*, January 1920 (as by Lewis Theobald).

UNTITLED: FOUR SEASONAL POEMS: *The Silver Clarion*, January 1919.

VERS RUSTICUM: *The Voice from the Mountain*, July 1918, in **LCL, Vol. IV** (q. v.).

VOICE, THE: *The Linnet*, August 1920; in **LCL, Vol. III** (q. v.).

VOLUNTEER, THE: *The Providence News*, February 1, 1918.

WELL, THE: *Phantagraph*, July 1937; *Weird Tales*, May 1944; included in **Dark of the Moon**, ed. August Derleth (Arkham House: Sauk City, 1947, pp xvi + 418, $3.00); in **Fungi from Yuggoth** (q. v.); in **Beyond the Wall of Sleep** (q. v.); in **Collected Poems** (q. v.).

WHERE ONCE POE WALKED: *Science-Fantasy Correspondent*, March-April, 1938 (*as* In a Sequestered Graveyard Where . . .); *Weird Tales,* May 1938; included in **The Man who Called Himself Poe**, ed. Sam Moskowitz (Doubleday: N. Y., 1969, pp 244, $4.95); (Gollancz: London, 1970, pp xvi + 240, £1.60); in **H. P. L.** (q. v.) (*as* In a Sequestered Graveyard Where . . .); in **Beyond the Wall of Sleep** (q. v.); in **Collected Poems** (q.v.).

WINDOW, THE: *Driftwind*, date unknown; *Weird Tales*, May 1944; in **Fungi from Yuggoth** (q. v.); in **Beyond the Wall of Sleep** (q. v.); in **Collected Poems** (q. v.); included in **Dark of the Moon**, ed. August Derleth (Arkham House: Sauk City, 1947, pp xvi + 418, $3.00).

WINTER WISH, A: *The Tryout*, February 1918.

WISDOM: *The Silver Clarion*, November 1919 (as by Archibald Maynwaring).

WOOD, THE: *The Tryout*, January 1927 (as by Lewis Theobald); *Weird Tales*, September 1938; in **H. P. L.** (q. v.); in **Beyond the Wall of Sleep** (q. v.); in **Collected Poems** (q. v.).

YE BALLADE OF PATRICK VON FLYNN: *The Conservative*, April 1916 (as by Theobald); in **LCL, Vol. IV** (q. v.).

YEAR OFF, A: in **Beyond the Wall of Sleep** (q. v.); in **Collected Poems** (q. v.).

YULE HORROR: *Weird Tales*, December 1926; in **Beyond the Wall of Sleep** (q. v.); in **Collected Poems** (q. v.).

ZAMAN'S HILL: *Driftwind*, October 1934; *Weird Tales*, February 1939; included in **Dark of the Moon**, ed. August Derleth (Arkham House: Sauk City, 1947, pp xvi + 418, $3.00); in **Fungi from Yuggoth** (q. v.); in **Beyond the Wall of Sleep** (q. v.); in **Collected Poems** (q. v.).

CHAPTER 3

Fiction

ALL AMATEUR publications covered here are English-language. English-language professional publications here covered are: *Amazing Stories*, *Arkham Collector*, *Arkham Sampler*, *Astounding Stories*, *Avon Fantasy Reader*, *Avon Science Fiction Reader*, *Bizarre Fantasy Tales*, *Bizarre Mystery Magazine*, *Edgar Wallace Mystery Magazine*, *Famous Fantastic Mysteries*, *Fantastic*, *Fantastic Novels*, *Fantasy and Science Fiction*, *Fresco*, *Home Brew*, *The London Evening Standard*, *Magazine of Horror*, *Marvel Tales*, *Mayfair Magazine*, *Rex Stout Mystery Magazine*, *Saturn Science Fiction*, *Startling Mystery Stories*, *Strange Tales*, *Tales of Magic and Mystery*, *True Supernatural Stories*, *Weird Tales*, and *Weird Terror Tales*.

The Italian-language publications here covered are: *I Giorni*, *I Racconti del Terrore*, *Pianeta*, *Storie di Fantasmi*, *Urania*, and *Week-End*.

The French-language publications here covered are: *Fiction*, *L'Herne*, *Les Lettres Nouvelles*, and *Planéte*.

The Polish-language publication here covered is: *Prze Kroj*.

ALCHEMIST, THE: *The United Amateur*, November 1916; in The Shuttered Room 1 (q. v.); in Dagon 1 (q. v.); in The Tomb (q. v.).

ARTHUR JERMYN: *Weird Tales*, April 1924 (as The White Ape); *Weird Tales*, May 1935; in The Outsider (q. v.); in The Lurking Fear 1 (q. v.); in The Lurking Fear 2 (q. v.); in Dagon 1 (q. v.); in Je Suis D'Ailleurs (q. v.).

AT THE MOUNTAINS OF MADNESS: *Astounding Stories*, February through April 1936; *I Giorni* #15, January 1966 as ''La Montagne della Follia''; included in Strange Ports of Call, ed. August Derleth (Pellegrini & Cudahy: N. Y., 1948, pp 393, $4.00); in The Outsider (q. v.); in At the Mountains of Madness 1 (q. v.); in At the Mountains of Madness 2 (q. v.); in Dans L'Abime du Temps (q. v.); in En Colo que Cayo del Cielo (q. v.).

AZATHOTH: *Leaves* II, 1938; in Marginalia (q. v.); in Dagon 1 (q. v.); in The Tomb (q. v.).

BATTLE THAT ENDED THE CENTURY, THE: Anonymously printed as a leaflet ca. 1935; *The Acolyte*, Fall 1944; included in Something About Cats (q. v.); *L'Herne* #12, April 1969. Almost certainly not entirely Lovecraft's work, perhaps not his at all. (He *did* deny authorship.).

BEAST IN THE CAVE, THE: *The Vagrant*, June 1918; *The Acolyte* #5, Fall 1943; in Marginalia (q. v.); in Dagon 1 (q. v.); in The Tomb (q. v.).

BEYOND THE WALL OF SLEEP: *Pine Cones*, October 1919, *The Fantasy Fan*, October 1934, *Weird Tales*, March 1938; *Avon Fantasy Reader* #6, 1948; included in The Other Side of the Moon, ed. August Derleth (Pellegrini & Cudahy: N. Y., 1949, pp 461, $3.75); (Grayson & Grayson: London, 1956, pp 238, $^{10}/_6$); (Panther: London, 1963, wpps 128, $^3/_6$); included in Legends for the Dark, ed. Peter Haining (Four Square: London, 1967, wpps 128, $^3/_6$); in Beyond the Wall of Sleep (q. v.); in Dagon 1 (q. v.); in Dagon 2 (q. v.); in The Doom that Came to Sarnath (q. v.); in Par Dela Le Mur du Sommiel (q. v.).

BOOK, THE: *Leaves* II, 1938; in **Marginalia** (q. v.); in **Dagon 1** (q. v.); in **The Tomb** (q. v.).

CALL OF CTHULHU, THE: *Weird Tales*, February 1928; *Storie di Fantasmi*, December 10, 1960, as "Il Richiano di Cthulhu"; included in **Beware After Dark**, ed. T. Everett Harre (Macauley: N. Y., 1929, pp 461, $2.50); (Gold Label: N. Y., 1931, $1.00): (Emerson: N. Y., 1942, 1945, $2.50); included in **Tales of the Cthulhu Mythos**, ed. August Derleth (Arkham House: Sauk City, 1969, pp 407, $7.50): (**Vol. One**: Beagle: N. Y. 95080, 1971, wpps 241, 95¢); in **The Outsider** (q. v.); in **Best Supernatural Stories** (q. v.); in **The Dunwich Horror 2** (q. v.); in **The Lurking Fear 1** (q. v.); in **The Haunter of the Dark** (q. v.); in **The Dunwich Horror 3** (q. v.); in **The Colour out of Space** (q. v.); in **Het Gefluister in de Duisternis** (q. v.); in **I Mostri All'angolo della Strada** (q. v.); in **Dans L'abime du Temps** (q. v.); in **En Colo que Cayo del Cielo** (q. v.).

CASE OF CHARLES DEXTER WARD, THE: *Weird Tales*, May and July 1941 (abridged); *I Giorni* #15, January 1966; included in **Night's Yawning Peal**, ed. August Derleth (Arkham House/Pellegrini & Cudahy: N. Y., 1952, pp 288, $3.00); in **Beyond the Wall of Sleep** (q. v.); in **At the Mountains of Madness 1** (q. v.); in **Par Dela le Mur du Sommiel** (q. v.); Victor Gollancz: London, 1952, pp 160, 9/6; Panther Books: London, 1963, 1965, wpps 127, 2/6; Belmont: N. Y., 1965, wpps 141, 50¢; Beagle: N. Y., 1971, wpps 127, 95¢.

CATS OF ULTHAR, THE: *The Tryout,* November 1920; *Weird Tales*, February 1926; *Weird Tales*, February 1933; as a pamphlet–Dragonfly Press: Cassia, Fla., 1935, wpps 10, 42 copy edition; *The Aonian*, Winter 1943; *Fantastic Novels*, January 1951; included in **The Young Magicians**, ed. Lin Carter (Ballantine: N. Y., 01730, 1969, wpps 280, 95¢); included in **Beware the Beasts**, ed. Vic Ghidalia & Roger Elwood (MacFadden: N. Y., 75-343, 1970, wpps 160, 75¢); in **The Outsider** (q. v.); in **Dagon 1** (q. v.); in **Dagon 2** (q. v.); in **The Doom that Came to Sarnath** (q. v.).

CELEPHAIS: *The Rainbow*, May 1922; *Marvel Tales*, May 1934; *Weird Tales*, June-July 1939; included in **The Garden of Fear & Other Stories**, ed. William C. Crawford (Crawford Pubs: L. A., 1945, wpps 79, 25¢); in **The Outsider** (q. v.); in **Dreams and Fancies** (q. v.); in **Dagon 1** (q. v.); in **Dagon 2** (q. v.); in **The Dream-Quest of Unknown Kadath** (q. v.).

COLOUR OUT OF SPACE, THE: *Amazing Stories*, September 1927; *Famous Fantastic Mysteries*, October 1941; *Urania* #310, June 10, 1963, as "Il Colore Venuto dal Cielo"; included in **The Night Side**, ed. August Derleth (Rinehart: N. Y., 1947, pp viii + 372, ill., $3.50): (Four Square Books: London, 1966, wpps 272, 5s); included in **The Omnibus of Science Fiction**, ed. Groff Conklin (Crown: N. Y., 1952, pp 562, $3.50): (as **Strange Travels in SF**: Grayson & Grayson: London, 1954, pp 256, 9/6) (as **SF Omnibus**: Berkeley: N. Y., G-31, 1956, wpps 187, 35¢); included in **Masterpieces of SF**, ed. Sam Moskowitz (World: N. Y., 1966, pp 552, $6.50); included in **Terror**, ed. Bryan A. Netherwood (Blackie: London, 1970, pp 384, 18s); included in **The Ghouls**, ed. Peter Haining (*as* **The Hollywood Nightmare**: Leslie Frewin: London, 1970, pp 382, 25s): (Stein & Day: N. Y., 1971, pp 382, $5.95): (a book club edition) *as* Monster of Terror; in **The Outsider** (q. v.); in **Best Supernatural Stories** (q. v.); in **The Dunwich Horror 2** (q. v.); in **The Lurking Fear 1** (q. v.); in **The Haunter of the Dark** (q. v.); in **The Dunwich Horror 3** (q. v.); in **The Colour out of Space** (q. v.); in **Three Tales of Horror** (q. v.); in **La Couleur Tombeé du Ciel** (q. v.); in **Makabere Verhalen** (q. v.); in **I Mostri All'-Angolo della Strada** (q. v.); in **En Colo que Cayo del Cielo** (q. v.); in **12 Grusel Stories** (q. v.).

COOL AIR: *Tales of Magic and Mystery*, March 1928; *Weird Tales*, September 1939; *Weird Tales* (British) 1944; *Strange Tales* #2 (1946); included in **Spine Chillers**, ed. Elisabeth Lee (Paul Elek Ltd.: London, 1961, pp 528, 25s); included in **Horror Times Ten**, ed. Alden H. Norton (Berkeley: N. Y., 1967, wpps 176, 60¢); in **The Outsider** (q. v.); in **Best Supernatural Stories** (q. v.); in **The Lurking Fear 1** (q. v.); in **The Dunwich Horror 3** (q. v.); in **The Colour out of Space** (q. v.); in **The Lurking Fear 2** (q. v.); in **The Shadow out of Time** (q. v.); in **I Mostri All'Angolo della Strada** (q. v.); in **Je suis D'Ailleurs** (q. v.); in **12 Grusel Stories** (q. v.).

DAGON: *The Vagrant*, November 1919; *Weird Tales*, October 1923; *Weird Tales*, January 1936; *Weird Tales*, November 1951; included in **Les Chefs D'Oeuvres de L'Epouvantes**, ed. Louis Pauwels and Jacques Bergier (Planéte: Paris, 1965, pp 500, 35F) as "Les Adorateurs du Fond de l'Abim"; in **The Outsider** (q. v.); in **The Shuttered Room 1** (q. v.); in **Dagon 1** (q. v.); in **Dagon 2** (q. v.); in **Makabere Verhalen** (q. v.); in **I Mostri All'Angolo Della Strada** (q. v.).

DESCENDANT, THE: *Leaves* II, 1938; in **Marginalia** (q. v.); in **Dagon** 1 (q. v.); in **The Tomb** (q. v.).

DOOM THAT CAME TO SARNATH, THE: *Scot*, June 1920; *Marvel Tales*, March-April 1935; *Weird Tales*, June 1938; *Kaleidoscope* II, November 1960; *Bizarre Fantasy Tales* #1, Fall 1970; included in **Swords and Sorcery**, ed. L. Sprague deCamp (Pyramid: N. Y., R-950, 1963, wpps 186, 50¢); in **Beyond the Wall of Sleep** (q. v.); in **Dreams and Fancies** (q. v.); in **Dagon** 1 (q. v.); in **Dagon** 2 (q. v.); in **The Doom that Came to Sarnath** (q. v.).

DREAM-QUEST OF UNKNOWN KADATH, THE: *The Arkham Sampler*, Winter through Autumn, 1948; *Weekend* #17, April 1967; in **Beyond the Wall of Sleep** (q. v.); in **At the Mountains of Madness** 1 (q. v.); in **The Dream-Quest of Unknown Kadath** (q. v.); in **At the Mountains of Madness** 2 (q. v.); in **Demons et Merveilles** 1 (q. v.); in **Demons et Merveilles** 2 (q. v.); alone—Shroud Publishers: Buffalo, N. Y., 1955, wpps 107, 1500 copy edition. According to various sources, including the publisher, 50 copies of the separate paperback were bound in hard covers and sold at $10 each. God only knows what the right number on the hardcover edition is, but it must be at least a hundred (150, at a guess).

DREAMS IN THE WITCH-HOUSE, THE: *Weird Tales*, July 1933; *Les Lettres Nouvelles* XXI, November 1954, *Magazine of Horror* #4, May 1964; *Week-End* #17, April 1967; included in **The Sleeping and the Dead**, ed. August Derleth (Pellegrini & Cudahy: N. Y., 1947, pp 578, ill., $3.75): (Four Square Books: London, 1963, wpps 253, ⅗); included in **Horror Omnibus**, ed. Kurt Singer (W. H. Allen: London, 1965, pp 317, 25s): (Panther: London 2158, 1966, wpps 283, 5s); included in **Great Untold Stories of Fantasy and Horror**, ed. Sam Moskowitz and Alden H. Norton (Pyramid: N. Y., T-2093, 1969, wpps 222, 75¢); in **The Outsider** (q. v.); in **At the Mountains of Madness** 1 (q. v.); in **At the Mountains of Madness** 2 (q. v.); in **Dans L'Abime du Temps** (q. v.).

DUNWICH HORROR, THE: *Weird Tales*, April 1929; *Storie di Fantasmi*, December 10, 1960 as "L'Orrore di Dunwich"; included in **Great Tales of Terror and the Supernatural**, ed. Herbert Wise and Phyllis Fraser (Random House: N.Y., 1944, pp xix + 1080, $2.95): (Random: Tor.): (Modern Library N. Y., 1947, pp xix + 1080, $2.45): (Hammond & Hammond: London, 1947, pp 382, 18s); included in **Avon Ghost Reader**, ed. Herbert Williams (Avon: N. Y., 90, 1946, wpps 258, 25¢); included in **Horror Stories**, ed. Elisabeth Lee (Bestseller Library: London, 1961, wpps 256, ⅖); (as **The Arrow Book of Horror Stories**: Arrow Books: London, 1962, 1965, wpps 256, 3s); included in **Eleven Great Horror Stories**, ed. Betty M. Owen (Scholastic Book Services: N. Y., TK1541, 1969, wpps 239, 60¢); in **The Outsider** (q. v.); in **Best Supernatural Stories** (q. v.); in **The Dunwich Horror** 1 (q. v.); in **The Dunwich Horror** 2 (q. v.); in **The Haunter of the Dark** (q. v.); in **The Dunwich Horror** 3 (q. v.); in **The Dunwich Horror** 4 (q. v.); in **Three Tales of Horror** (q. v.); in **I Mostri All'Angolo della Strada** (q. v.); in **La Couleur Tombée du Ciel** (q. v.); in **12 Grusel Stories** (q. v.).

EVIL CLERGYMAN, THE: *Weird Tales*, April 1939 (as "The Wicked Clergyman"); in **Beyond the Wall of Sleep** (q. v.); in **Dreams and Fancies** (q. v.); in **Dagon** 1 (q. v.); in **The Tomb** (q. v.).

EX OBLIVIONE: *The United Amateur*, March 1921 (as by Ward Phillips); *The Phantagraph*, July 1937; *Magazine of Horror* #24, November 1968; included in **Operation Phantasy**, ed. Donald A. Wollheim (Phantagraph Press: Rego Park, N. Y., 1967, pp 59, $4.00); in **Beyond the Wall of Sleep** (q. v.); in **The Doom that Came to Sarnath** (q. v.); alone—Roy A. Squires: Glendale, Calif., 1969, wpps 16, $5.00, 125 copy edition. The separate edition is the second of a set of four gorgeously-printed booklets. As is usual with Roy Squires, his name appears nowhere on the booklet. Would that we all could get along that well on reputation!

FESTIVAL, THE: *Weird Tales*, January 1925; *Weird Tales*, October 1933; *Edgar Wallace Mystery Magazine* #1, March 1966; included in **The Satanists**, ed. Peter Haining (Neville Spearman: London, 1969, pp 249, 18s): (Taplinger: N. Y., 1970, pp 249, $5.95): (Pyramid: N. Y., N2640, 1972, wpps 255, 95¢).

FROM BEYOND: *The Fantasy Fan*, June 1934; *Weird Tales*, February 1938; *Mayfair Magazine*, December 1969; included in **Worlds of Tomorrow**, ed. August Derleth (Pellegrini & Cudahy: N. Y., 1953, pp 351, $3.95): (as **New Worlds for Old**: Four Square: London, 1964, wpps 122, ⅖); in **Beyond the Wall of Sleep** (q. v.); in **Dagon** 1 (q. v.); in **The Doom that Came to Sarnath** (q. v.); in **Dagon** 2 (q. v.); in **Makabere Verhalen** (q. v.).

FROM THE DARK: *see* Herbert West—Reanimator.

GREWSOME TALES: *see* Herbert West—Reanimator.

HAUNTER OF THE DARK, THE: *Weird Tales*, December 1936, included in **Terror at Night**, ed. Herbert Williams (Avon: N. Y., 110, 1947, wpps 194, 25¢); included in **Bodies and Spirits**, ed. Dan Herr and Joel Wells (Doubleday: N. Y., 1964, pp 192, $.); included in **Medley Macabre**, ed. Bryan A. Nethewood (Hammond & Hammond: London, 1966, pp 544, 30s); included in **The Boris Karloff Horror Anthology** (Souvenir Press: London, 1965, pp 190, 21s); (Corgi: London GN762, 1967, wpps 158, 3/6); (*as* **Boris Karloff's Favorite Horror Stories**: Avon: N. Y., G1254, 1965, wpps 176, 50¢); in **Tales of the Cthulhu Mythos**, ed. August Derleth (Arkham House: Sauk City, 1969, pp 407, $7.50); (Vol. Two: Beagle: N. Y., 95124, 1971, wpps 277, 95¢); in **The Outsider** (q.v.); in **Best Supernatural Stories** (q.v.); in **Haunter of the Dark** (q.v.); in **Dunwich Horror 3** (q.v.); in **Dunwich Horror 4** (q.v.); in **Makabere Verhalen** (q.v.); in **I Nostri All'Angolo della Strada** (q.v.); in **Par dela le Mur du Sommiel** (q.v.); in **12 Grusel Stories** (q.v.).

HE: *Weird Tales*, September 1926, *Weird Terror Tales* #1, Winter 1969; included in **Terror in the Modern Vein**, ed. Donald A. Wollheim (Hanover House: N. Y., 1955, pp 315, $3.95): (Digit: London, R460, 1961, wpps 156, 2/6); in **The Outsider** (q.v.); in **The Weird Shadow over Innsmouth** (q.v.); in **Dagon 1** (q.v.); in **The Tomb** (q.v.); in **Makabere Verhalen** (q.v.).

HERBERT WEST–REANIMATOR: *Home Brew*, February to July 1922 (six parts; the first six issues of the magazine) under the heading of "Grewsome Tales" with these subtitles: *From the Dark/The Plague Demon/Six Shots by Moonlight/The Scream of the Dead/The Horror from the Shadows/The Tomb-Legions*; *Weird Tales* (same subtitles), March, July, September, November 1942 and September, November 1943; in **Beyond the Wall of Sleep** (q.v.); in **Dagon 1** (q.v.); in **Dagon 2** (q.v.); in **I Mostri All'Angolo della Strada** (q.v.).

HORROR AT RED HOOK, THE: *Weird Tales*, January 1927; *Weird Tales*, March 1952; *Bizarre Mystery Magazine*, October 1965; included in **You'll Need A Nightlight**, ed. Christine Campbell Thomson (Selwyn Blount: London, 1927, pp 254, 2s); included in **Not at Night!**, ed. by Herbert Asbury (Macy-Masius: The Vanguard Press: N. Y., 1928, pp 286); included in **When Evil Wakes**, ed. August Derleth (Souvenir Press: London, 1963, pp 288, 18s): (Corgi: London, 1964, wpps 223, 3/6); included in **Fright**, ed. Charles M. Collins (Avon: N. Y., 1963, wpps 141, 50¢); included in **Horor 1**, ed. Maurizio Belloti (Sugar: Rome, 1965); in **The Outsider** (q.v.); in **Dagon 1** (q.v.); in **The Tomb** (q.v.).

HORROR FROM THE SHADOWS, THE: *see* Herbert West–Reanimator.

HOUND, THE: *Weird Tales*, February 1925; *Weird Tales*, September 1929; in **Beyond the Wall of Sleep** (q.v.); in **The Dunwich Horror 2** (q.v.); in **The Lurking Fear 1** (q.v.); in **The Lurking Fear 2** (q.v.); in **Dagon 1** (q.v.); in **Je Suis D'Ailleurs** (q.v.).

HYPNOS: *The National Amateur*, May 1923; *Weird Tales*, May-June-July 1924; *Weird Tales*, November 1937; *Planéte* #1, October-November 1961; included in **Les 20 Meilleurs Recits de SF**, ed. Herbert Juin (Marabout: Verviers, Belgium, 1964, wpps 445, 4.65Fr); in **The Outsider** (q.v.); in **Dagon 1** (q.v.); in **The Doom that Came to Sarnath** (q.v.); in **Dagon 2** (q.v.).

IMPRISONED WITH THE PHARAOHS: *Weird Tales*, May-June-July 1924 (as by Houdini); *Weird Tales*, June-July 1939; in **Marginalia** (q.v.); in **Dagon 1** (q.v.); in **The Tomb** (q.v.); in **The Doom that Came to Sarnath** (q.v.).

IN THE VAULT: *The Tryout*, November 1925; *Weird Tales*, April 1932; *Storie di Fantasmi* December 10, 1960 *as* "Nella Cripta"; *L'Herne* #12, April 1969; included in **In the Grip of Terror**, ed. Groff Conklin (Perma Books: N. Y., P117, 1951, wpps 364, 25¢); included in **Hauntings: Tales of the Supernatural**, ed. Henry Mazzeo (Doubleday: N. Y., 1968, pp 319, $4.50); in **The Outsider** (q.v.); in **Best Supernatural Stories** (q.v.); in **The Dunwich Horror 2** (q.v.); in **The Dunwich Horror 3** (q.v.); in **The Colour out of Space** (q.v.); in **The Lurking Fear 2** (q.v.); in **The Shadow out of Time** (q.v.); in **I Mostri All'Angolo della Strada** (q.v.); in **12 Grusel Stories** (q.v.).

LITTLE GLASS BOTTLE, The: in **The Shuttered Room 1** (q.v.).

LURKING FEAR, THE: *Home Brew*, January through April 1923 (four parts); *Weird Tales*, June 1928; *Startling Mystery Stories* #1, Summer 1966; in **The Outsider** (q.v.); in **The Lurking Fear 1** (q.v.); in **The Lurking Fear 2** (q.v.); in **Dagon 1** (q.v.); in **Je suis D'Ailleurs** (q.v.).

MEMORY: *The United Co-operative*, June 1919 (as by Lewis Theobald); *Magazine of Horror* #24, November 1968; *L'Herne* #12, April 1969; in **Beyond the Wall of Sleep** (q.v.); in **Dreams and Fancies** (q.v.); in **The Doom that Came to Sarnath** (q.v.); alone—Roy A. Squires: Glendale, Calif., 1969, wpps 16, $5.00, 125 copy edition. The separate edition is the first of a series of four booklets.

MONSTER OF TERROR: *see* The Colour out of Space.

MOON-BOG, THE: *Weird Tales*, June 1926; included in **The Wild Night Company**, ed. Peter Haining (Victor Gollancz: London, 1970, pp 288, 36s); in **Beyond the Wall of Sleep** (q.v.); in **The Dunwich Horror 2** (q.v.); in **The Lurking Fear 1** (q.v.); in **The Lurking Fear 2** (q.v.); in **Dagon 1** (q.v.); in **Je Suis D'Ailleurs** (q.v.).

MUSIC OF ERICH ZANN, THE: *The National Amateur*, March 1922; *Weird Tales*, May 1925; *The London Evening Standard*, October 24, 1932; *Weird Tales*, November 1934; *Famous Fantastic Mysteries*, March 1951; *Fresco*, Spring 1958; *Fiction*, 1958; *Pianeta* #7, April-May 1965 as "La Musica di Erich Zann"; included in **Creeps by Night**, ed. Dashiell Hammett (John Day: N. Y., 1931, pp xv + 525, $2.50): (as **Modern Tales of Horror**: Gollancz: London, 1932, pp 448, 5s): (Blue Ribbon Books: N. Y., 1936, pp 525, $1.00): (McClelland: Tor. $1.29): (World: N. Y., 1944, pp 525, $1.00): (as **The Red Brain**: Belmont: N. Y., 1961, wpps 141, 50¢): (as **The Red Brain**: New English Library: London, 1965, wpps 159, ³/₆): included in **The Short Story**, ed. James B. Hall and Joseph Langland (MacMillan: N. Y., 1956, pp 485); in **The Outsider** (q.v.); in **Best Supernatural Stories** (q.v.); in **The Dunwich Horror 2** (q.v.); in **The Haunter of the Dark** (q.v.); in **The Dunwich Horror 3** (q.v.); in **The Dunwich Horror 4** (q.v.); in **Het Gefluister in de Duisternis** (q.v.); in **I Mostri All'Angolo della Strada** (q.v.); in **Je suis D'Ailleurs** (q.v.).

MYSTERIOUS SHIP, THE: in **The Shuttered Room 1** (q.v.).

MYSTERY OF THE GRAVEYARD, THE: in **The Shuttered Room 1** (q.v.).

NAMELESS CITY, THE: *Transatlantic Circular*, 1920's; *Fanciful Tales* #1, Fall 1936; *Weird Tales*, November 1938; in **The Outsider** (q.v.); in **The Lurking Fear 1** (q.v.); in **The Lurking Fear 2** (q.v.); in **Dagon 1** (q.v.); in **The Doom that Came to Sarnath** (q.v.); in **Je Suis D'Ailleurs** (q.v.).

NYARLATHOTEP: *The United Amateur*, November 1920; *The National Amateur*, July 1926; *Supermundane Stories*, Spring 1938; *Fiction*, March 1969; *L'Herne* #12, April 1969; *Magazine of Horror* #24, November 1969; *The Arkham Collector* #6, Winter 1970; included in **The World's Shortest Stories**, ed. Richard C. Hubler (Duell, Sloan & Pearce: N. Y., 1961, pp 268); in **Beyond the Wall of Sleep** (q.v.); in **Dreams and Fancies** (q.v.); in **The Doom that Came to Sarnath** (q.v.); in **I Mostri All'Angolo della Strada** (q.v.); alone—Roy A. Squires: Glendale, Calif., 1969, wpps 20, $5.00, 125 copy edition. The separate edition is the third of a series of four booklets.

OLD BUGS: in **The Shuttered Room 1** (q.v.). Extraction from a letter to Alfred Galpin.

OTHER GODS, THE: *The Fantasy Fan*, November 1933; *True Supernatural Stories*, October 1934; *Weird Tales*, October 1938; included in **The Fantastic Swordsmen**, ed. L. Sprague de Camp (Pyramid: N. Y., 1967, wpps 204, 60¢); in **Beyond the Wall of Sleep** (q.v.); in **Dagon 1** (q.v.); in **The Doom that Came to Sarnath** (q.v.); in **Dagon 2** (q.v.).

OUTSIDER, THE: *Weird Tales*, April 1926; *Weird Tales*, June-July 1931; *Famous Fantastic Mysteries*, June 1950; *Fiction*, 1956; *Fiction*, 1958; *Startling Mystery Stories* #14, Winter 1969; included in **The Complete Murder Sampler**, ed. James Nelson (Crime Club/Doubleday: N. Y., 1946, pp xii + 368); included in **The Graveyard Reader**, ed. Groff Conklin (Ballantine: N. Y., 1958, wpps 188, 35¢; 1965, wpps 156, 50¢); included in **Spine Chillers**, ed. Elizabeth Lee (Paul Elek Ltd: London, 1961, pp 528, 25s); included in **Famous Monster Tales**, ed. Basil Davenport (Van Nostrand: Princeton, N. J., 1967, pp 201); included in **Les Chefs D'Oeuvres du Fantastique**, ed. Louis Pauwels, Jacques Bergier, Jacques Sternberg, and Alex Grail (Planéte: Paris, 1967, pp 480, 45Fr) *as* "Celui d'Autre-part"; included in **The Unspeakable People**, ed. Peter Haining (Leslie Frewin: London, 1969, pp 246, 30s); (Popular Library: N. Y., 01376, 1970, wpps 207, 75¢); in **The Outsider** (q.v.); in **The Weird Shadow over Innsmouth** (q.v.); in **Best Supernatural Stories** (q.v.); in **The Dunwich Horror 2** (q.v.); in **The Haunter of the Dark** (q.v.); in **The Dunwich Horror 3** (q.v.); in **The Colour out of Space** (q.v.); in **The Shuttered Room 1** (q.v.); in **Het Gefluister in de Duisternis** (q.v.); in **I Mostri All'Angolo della Strada** (q.v.); in **Je Suis D'Ailleurs** (q.v.); in **12 Grusel Stories** (q.v.).

PICKMAN'S MODEL: *Weird Tales*, October 1927; *Weird Tales*, November 1936; *Famous Fantastic Mysteries*, December 1951; *Urania* #310, June 10, 1963 *as* "Il Modello di Pickman"; included in By Daylight Only, ed. Christine Campbell Thomson (Selwyn Blount: London, 1929, pp 288, 2s); included in Not at Night Omnibus, ed. Christine Campbell Thomson (Selwyn Blount: London, 1937, pp 510, ³⁄₆); in The Outsider (q. v.); in Best Supernatural Stories (q. v.); in The Dunwich Horror 2 (q. v.); in The Lurking Fear 1 (q. v.); in The Haunter of the Dark (q. v.); in The Dunwich Horror 3 (q. v.); in The Dunwich Horror 4 (q. v.); in Het Gefluister in de Duisternis (q. v.); in I Mostri All'Angolo della Strada (q. v.); in Je suis D'Ailleurs (q. v.); in 12 Grusel Stories (q. v.).

PICTURE IN THE HOUSE, THE: *The National Amateur*, July 1919; *Weird Tales*, January 1924; *Weird Tales*, March 1937; *L'Herne* #12, April 1969, in The Outsider (q. v.); in Best Supernatural Stories (q. v.); in The Dunwich Horror 3 (q. v.); in The Colour out of Space (q. v.); in The Lurking Fear 2 (q. v.); in The Shadow out of Time (q. v.); in 12 Grusel Stories (q. v.).

PLAGUE DEMON, THE: *see* Herbert West—Reanimator.

POLARIS: *The Philosopher*, December 1920; *The Fantasy Fan*, February 1934; *Weird Tales*, December 1937; in The Outsider (q. v.); in Dagon 1 (q. v.); in The Doom that Came to Sarnath (q. v.); in Dagon 2 (q. v.).

QUEST OF IRANON, THE: *The Galleon*, July-August 1935; *Weird Tales*, March 1939; *Mirage V*, Spring 1962; included in The Young Magicians, ed. Lin Carter (Ballantine: N. Y., 01730, 1969, wpps 280, 95¢); in Beyond the Wall of Sleep (q. v.); in Dagon 1 (q. v.); in The Doom that Came to Sarnath (q. v.).

RATS IN THE WALLS, THE: *Weird Tales*, March 1924; *Weird Tales*, June 1930; *Rex Stout Mystery Magazine* III, February 1946; *I Racconti del Terrore* #3-4, August-September 1962; included in Switch on the Light, ed. Christine Campbell Thomson (Selwyn Blount: London, 1931, pp 256, 2s); included in Sleep no More, ed. August Derleth (Rinehart: N. Y., 1944, pp 374, ill., $2.50): (Armed Services edition: N. Y., 1944, np); included in Great Tales of Terror and the Supernatural, ed. Herbert Wise and Phyllis Frazer (Random House: N. Y., 1944, pp xix + 1080, $2.95): (Random: Tor.): (Modern Library: N. Y., 1947, pp xix + 1080, $2.45): (Hammond & Hammond: London, 1947, pp 832, 18s); included in Griezelverhalen, ed. A. De Bruyn and

A. Van der Hoek (Het Spectrum: Antwerp, 1958, wpps , . Fr); *as* "De Ratten"; included in Un Secolo di Terrore, ed. Bruno Tasso (Sugar: Rome, 1960, wpps , lire): as "I Topi nel Muro"; included in Il Breviaro del Brivido, ed. Bruno Tasso (Sugar: Rome, 1967, wpps , lire); in The Outsider (q. v.); in Best Supernatural Stories (q. v.); in The Dunwich Horror 2 (q. v.); in The Haunter of the Dark (q. v.); in The Dunwich Horror 3 (q. v.); in The Dunwich Horror 4 (q. v.); in I Mostri All'Angolo della Strada (q. v.); in Par dela le Mur du Sommiel (q. v.).

SCREAM OF THE DEAD, THE: *see* Herbert West—Reanimator.

SECRET CAVE, THE: in The Shuttered Room 1 (q. v.).

SHADOW OUT OF TIME, THE: *Astounding Stories*, June 1936; included in The Portable Novels of Science, ed. Donald A. Wollheim (Viking: N. Y., 1945, pp 737, $2.00); in The Outsider (q. v.); in The Dunwich Horror 1 (q. v.); in Dreams and Fancies (q. v.); in The Dunwich Horror 3 (q. v.); in The Lurking Fear 2 (q. v.); in The Shadow out of Time (q. v.); in Dans L'Abime du Temps (q. v.).

SHADOW OVER INNSMOUTH, THE: *Weird Tales*, January 1942 (Canadian edition, March 1942); *Prze Kroj* #766-768, 1959; included in Universo a Sette Incognite, ed. Sarah Cantoni (Mondadori: Milan, 1963, wpps , lire) *as* "La Maschera di Innsmouth"; in The Outsider (q. v.); in The Weird Shadow over Innsmouth (q. v.); in The Dunwich Horror 2 (q. v.); in The Dunwich Horror 3 (q. v.); in The Lurking Fear 2 (q. v.); in The Shadow out of Time (q. v.); in I Mostri All'Angolo della Strada (q. v.); in La Couleur Tombée du Ciel (q. v.); in 12 Grusel Stories (q. v.).

SHUNNED HOUSE, THE: *Weird Tales*, October 1937; *I Giorni* #15, January 1966 as "La Casa Sfuggita"; included in Who Knocks?, ed. August Derleth (Rinehart: N. Y., 1946, pp 191, ill., $3.00); included in Twisted, ed. Groff Conklin (Belmont: N. Y., 1962, wpps 189, 50¢): (New English Library: London, 1965, wpps 224, ³⁄₆); in The Outsider (q. v.); in The Lurking Fear 1 (q. v.); in At the Mountains of Madness 1 (q. v.); in The Lurking Fear 2 (q. v.); in Je suis D'Ailleurs (q. v.).

SILVER KEY, THE: *Weird Tales*, January 1929; *Avon Fantasy Reader* III, 1947; *Week-End* #17, April 1967; in The Outsider (q. v.); in At the Mountains of Madness 1 (q. v.); in The Dream-Quest of Unknown Kadath (q. v.); in At the Mountains of Madness 2 (q. v.); in Demons et Merveilles 1 (q. v.).

SIX SHOTS BY MOONLIGHT: *see* Herbert West—Reanimator.

STATEMENT OF RANDOLPH CARTER, THE: *The Vagrant*, May 1920; *Weird Tales*, February 1925; *Weird Tales*, August 1937; *Avon Fantasy Reader* X, 1949; in *I Giorni* #15, January 1966; included in Shapes of the Supernatural, ed. Seon Manley and Gogo Lewis (Doubleday: N. Y., 1969, pp x + 370, ill., $5.95); in The Outsider (q.v.); in At the Mountains of Madness 1 (q.v.); in At the Mountains of Madness 2 (q.v.); in Demons et Merveilles 1 (q.v.).

STRANGE HIGH HOUSE IN THE MIST, THE: *Weird Tales*, October 1931; included in Weird Tales, ed. Leo Margulies (Pyramid: N. Y., R-1029, 1964, wpps 155, 50¢); in The Outsider (q.v.); in The Shuttered Room 1 (q.v.); in Dagon 1 (q.v.); in The Dream-Quest of Unknown Kadath (q.v.); in The Tomb (q.v.).

THE STREET: *The Wolverine*, December 1920; *The National Amateur*, January 1922; in The Shuttered Room 1 (q.v.); in Dagon 1 (q.v.); in The Tomb (q.v.).

SWEET ERMENGARDE: in Beyond the Wall of Sleep (q.v.); *Mirage* #7.

TEMPLE, THE: *Weird Tales*, September 1925; *Weird Tales*, February 1936; *Avon Fantasy Reader* VIII, 1948; *Pianeta* #2, May-June 1964 as ''Il Tempio''; included in Hauntings and Horrors, ed. Alden H. Norton (Berkeley: N. Y., X1674, 1969, wpps 171, 60¢); in The Outsider (q.v.); in Dagon 1 (q.v.); in Dagon 2 (q.v.); in Makabere Verhalen (q.v.).

TERRIBLE OLD MAN, THE: *The Tryout*, July 1921; *Weird Tales*, August 1926; *L'Herne* #12, April 1969; in The Outsider (q.v.); in Best Supernatural Stories (q.v.); in The Dunwich Horror 3 (q.v.); in The Colour out of Space (q.v.); in The Lurking Fear 2 (q.v.); in The Shadow Out of Time (q.v.); in 12 Grusel Stories (q.v.).

THING IN THE MOONLIGHT, THE: *Bizarre*, January 1941; *The Arkham Collector* #4, Winter 1969; in Marginalia (q.v.); in Dreams and Fancies (q.v.); in Dagon 1 (q.v.); in The Tomb (q.v.).

THING ON THE DOORSTEP, THE: *Weird Tales*, January 1937; included in And the Darkness Falls, ed. Boris Karloff (World: N. Y., 1946, pp 631, $2.75); included in Voor en na Middernacht, ed. B.

Jessurun Lobo (Elsevièr: Antwerp, 1954, pp   , as ''Het Ding op de Drempel''; included in The Macabre Reader, ed. Donald A. Wollheim (Ace: N. Y., D-353, 1959, wpps 223, 35¢); (Digit: London, D362, 1960, wpps 188, 2s); included in Spine Chillers, ed. Elisabeth Lee (Paul Elek: London, 1961, pp 528, 25s); included in Best Horror Stories, Vol. Two, ed. John Kier Cross (Faber & Faber: London, 1965, pp 270, 18s); included in The Unhumans, ed. Marvin Allen Kays (Popular Library: N. Y., 1965, wpps 141, 50¢); in The Outsider (q.v.); in Best Supernatural Stories (q.v.); in The Dunwich Horror 1 (q.v.); in The Haunter of the Dark (q.v.); in The Dunwich Horror 3 (q.v.); in The Dunwich Horror 4 (q.v.); in Three Tales of Horror (q.v.); in I Mostri All'Angolo della Strada (q.v.); in Par dela le Mur du Sommiel (q.v.); in 12 Grusel Stories (q.v.).

TOMB, THE: *The Vagrant*, March 1922; *Weird Tales*, January 1926; included in Tales of the Undead, ed. Elinore Blaisdell (Thomas Crowell: N. Y., 1947, pp 372, $3.50); (Oxford: Tor. $3.50); in The Outsider (q.v.); in Dagon 1 (q.v.); in The Tomb (q.v.); in The Doom that Came to Sarnath (q.v.).

TOMB-LEGIONS, THE: *see* Herbert West—Reanimator.

TRANSITION OF JUAN ROMERO, THE: in Marginalia (q.v.); in Dagon 1 (q.v.); in The Tomb (q.v.).

TREE, THE: *The Tryout*, October 1921; *Weird Tales*, August 1938; in Beyond the Wall of Sleep (q.v.); in Dagon 1 (q.v.); in The Doom that Came to Sarnath (q.v.); in Dagon 2 (q.v.).

UNNAMABLE, THE: *The Vagrant*, 1920's; *Weird Tales*, July 1925; in Beyond the Wall of Sleep (q.v.); in The Lurking Fear 1 (q.v.); in The Lurking Fear 2 (q.v.); in Dagon 1 (q.v.); in Je suis D'Ailleurs (q.v.).

VERY OLD FOLK, THE: *Scienti-Snaps*, Summer 1940, in Marginalia (q.v.).

WHAT THE MOON BRINGS: *The National Amateur*, May 1923; *Cosmic Tales* #15, April-May-June 1941; *Magazine of Horror* #24, November 1968; in Beyond the Wall of Sleep (q.v.); in The Doom that Came to Sarnath (q.v.); alone—Roy A. Squires: Glendale, Calif., 1970, wpps 20, $5.00, 125 copy edition. The separate edition is the last of a series of four booklets.

WHISPERER IN DARKNESS, THE: *Weird Tales*, August
1931; *Urania* #310, June 16, 1963; included in
Strange Signposts, ed. Sam Moskowitz and Roger
Elwood (Holt, Rinehart & Winston: N. Y., 1966,
pp 351, $5.95); included in The Spawn of Cthulhu,
ed. Lin Carter (Ballantine: N. Y., 02394, 1971,
wpps 274, 95¢); in The Outsider (q.v.); in Weird
Shadow over Innsmouth (q.v.); in Best Supernatural
Stories (q.v.); in The Dunwich Horror 2 (q.v.); in
The Haunter of the Dark (q.v.); in The Dunwich
Horror 3 (q.v.); in The Colour out of Space (q.
v.); in En Colo que Cayo del Cielo (q.v.); in Het
Gefluister in de Duisternis (q.v.); in I Mostri
All'Angolo della Strada (q.v.); in La Couleur
Tombée du Ciel (q.v.); in 12 Grusel Stories (q.v.).

WHITE APE, THE: *see* Arthur Jermyn.

WHITE SHIP, THE: *The United Amateur*, November
1919; *Weird Tales*, March 1927; in Beyond the
Wall of Sleep (q.v.); in Dagon 1 (q.v.); in The
Dream-Quest of Unknown Kadath (q.v.); in Dagon
1 (q.v.); in Dagon 2 (q.v.).

WICKED CLERGYMAN, THE: *see* The Evil Clergyman.

Collaborations

with ANNA HELEN CROFTS

POETRY AND THE GODS: *The United Amateur*, September 1920 (as by Crofts and Henry Paget-Lowe); in The Shuttered Room 1 (q. v.); in Dagon 1 (q. v.); in The Tomb (q. v.).

with AUGUST DERLETH

ANCESTOR, THE: original in The Survivor and Others (q. v.); included in Beyond the Curtain of Dark, ed. Peter Haining (Four Square: London, 1966, wpps 320, 5s); in The Shuttered Room 2 (q. v.); in The Shadow Out of Time (q. v.).

DARK BROTHERHOOD, THE: original in The Dark Brotherhood (q. v.); included in The Man Who Called Himself Poe, ed. Sam Moskowitz (Doubleday: N. Y., 1969, pp 244, $4.95); (Gollancz: London, 1970, pp 244, 21s); in The Shuttered Room 2 (q. v.); in The Shadow Out of Time (q. v.); in The Shuttered Room 3 (q. v.).

FISHERMAN OF FALCON POINT, THE: original in The Shuttered Room 1 (q. v.); in The Shadow Out of Time (q. v.); in The Shuttered Room 2 (q. v.); in The Shuttered Room 3 (q. v.).

GABLE WINDOW, THE: *Saturn*, May 1957; as "The Murky Glass"; included in Wie Kan ik Zeggen Dat Er Is?, ed. anonymous (Brunau: Amsterdam, 1968, pp   , *f*   .); in The Survivor and Others (q. v.); in The Shuttered Room 2 (q. v.); in The Shadow Out of Time (q. v.); in I Mostri All'Angolo Della Strada (q. v.).

HORROR FROM THE MIDDLE SPAN, THE: original in Travellers By Night, ed. August Derleth (Arkham House: Sauk City, 1967, pp 261, $4.00); in The Shuttered Room 3 (q. v.).

LAMP OF ALHAZRED, THE: *F&SF*, October 1957, Wie Kan Ik Zeggen Dat Er Is?, ed. Anonymous (Brunau: Amsterdam, 1968, pp   , *f*   .); as

"De Lamp van Alhazred"; in The Survivor and Others (q. v.); in The Shuttered Room 2 (q. v.); in The Shadow Out of Time (q. v.).

LURKER AT THE THRESHOLD, THE: Arkham House: Sauk City, 1945, pp 196, $2.50; Museum Press: London, 1948, pp 224, ⁵⁄₆; Panther: London, 1970, wpps 160, 25p; Beagle: N. Y., 1971, wpps 160, 95¢.

PEABODY HERITAGE, THE: original in The Survivor and Others (q. v.); included in The Evil People, ed. Peter Haining (Leslie Frewin: London, 1968, pp 352, 18s); (Popular Library: N. Y., 1969, wpps 241, 75¢); included in Histoires D'Outre-Monde, ed. Jacques Papy (Casterman: Antwerp, 1966, 337, 135 fr.) as "La Chambre Secrete"; included in Wie Kan Ik Zeggen Dat Er Is?, ed. Anonymous (Brunau: Amsterdam, 1968, pp   ,   ) as "Erfenis van Peabody"; in The Shadow Out of Time (q. v.); in The Shuttered Room 2 (q. v.).

SHADOW IN THE ATTIC, THE: original in Over the Edge, ed. August Derleth (Arkham House: Sauk City, 1964, pp vi + 297, $5.00); in The Shuttered Room 3 (q. v.).

SHADOW OUT OF SPACE, THE: original in The Survivor and Others (q. v.); in *Fantastic*, February 1962; in The Shuttered Room 2 (q. v.); in The Shadow Out of Time (q. v.).

SHUTTERED ROOM, THE: original in The Shuttered Room 1 (q. v.); included in When Evil Wakes, ed. August Derleth (Souvenir Press: London, 1963, pp 288, 18s); (Corgi: London,   , 1964, wpps   ,   ); *Magazine of Horror* #7, January 1965, included in The Third Fontana Book of Ghost Stories, ed. Christine Bernard (Fontana: London,   , 1968, wpps 192, ³⁄₆); (Berkeley: N. Y.,   , 1971, wpps 192, 75¢); included in Wie Kan Ik Zeggen Dat Er Is?, ed. anonymous (Brunau: Amsterdam, 1968, pp   ,   ); included in Histoires Insolites, ed. M. Roth and others (Casterman: Antwerp, 1964, pp 368, 13.50 fr) as "La Chambre aux Volets Clos"; in The Shuttered Room 2 (q. v.); in The Shuttered Room 3 (q. v.); in The Shadow Out of Time (q. v.).

SURVIVOR, THE: *Weird Tales*, July 1954; included in Beyond the Curtain of Dark, ed. Peter Haining (Four Square: London,   , 1966, wpps 320, 5s); in The Survivor and Others (q.v.); in The Shuttered Room 2 (q.v.); in The Shadow Out of Time (q.v.).

WENTWORTH'S DAY: original in The Survivor and Others (q.v.); included in Histoires D'Outre Monde, ed. Jacques Papy (Casterman: Antwerp, 1966, pp 337, 135 fr) as "L'Echeange"; in The Shuttered Room 2 (q.v.); in The Shadow Out of Time (q.v.).

WITCHES' HOLLOW: original in Dark Mind, Dark Heart, ed. August Derleth (Arkham House: Sauk City, 1962, pp 249, $4.00); (Mayflower: London,   , 1963, wpps 222, ⅜); in The Shuttered Room 3 (q.v.).

with WINIFRED J. JACKSON

CRAWLING CHAOS, THE: *The United Amateur*, 1920, (as by Lewis Theobald, Jr. and Elizabeth Neville Berkeley); *Tesseract*, April and May, 1937; *Tesseract Annual*, 1939; *United Co-operative*, April 1921; in Beyond the Wall of Sleep (q.v.); in The Horror in the Museum (q.v.); in The Doom that Came to Sarnath (q.v.).

GREEN MEADOW, THE: *The Vagrant*, Spring 1927 (as by Lewis Theobald, Jr. and Elizabeth Neville Berkeley; in Beyond the Wall of Sleep (q.v.); in The Horror in the Museum (q.v.).

with C. L. MOORE, A. MERRITT, ROBERT E. HOWARD, and FRANK BELKNAP LONG, Jr.

CHALLENGE FROM BEYOND, THE: *Fantasy Magazine*, September 1935; as a pamphlet—Pennsylvania Dutch Cheese Press: Washington, D. C., 1954, wpps 12, about 75 copies done; included in Horrors Unknown, ed. Sam Moskowitz (Walker: N.Y., 1971, pp 214, $5.95); (Kaye & Ward: London, 1972, pp 214, £1.65); in Beyond the Wall of Sleep (q.v.). The Lovecraft portion was reprinted alone in *Fantastic*, May 1960.

with E. HOFFMAN PRICE

THROUGH THE GATES OF THE SILVER KEY: *Weird Tales*, July 1934; *Avon Fantasy Reader* XVII, 1951; *Week-End* #17, April 1967, as "Attraverso le Porte della Chiave d'Argento"; in The Outsider (q.v.); in At the Mountains of Madness 1 (q.v.); in At the Mountains of Madness 2 (q.v.); in The Dream-Quest of Unknown Kadath (q.v.); in Demons et Merveilles 1 (q.v.); in Demons et Merveilles 2 (q.v.).

with KENNETH STERLING

IN THE WALLS OF ERYX: *Weird Tales*, October 1939; *Avon Science Fiction Reader* III, 1952; in Beyond the Wall of Sleep (q.v.); in Dagon 1 (q.v.); in The Tomb (q.v.); in The Doom that Came to Sarnath (q.v.).

CHAPTER 4

Collections

AT THE MOUNTAINS OF MADNESS & OTHER NOVELS: (**At the Mountains of Madness 1**)—Arkham House: Sauk City, 1964, pp xi + 432, $6.50. Reprinted 1968 at $7.50. Editions of about 3000 copies each; the dust jacket (by Lee Brown Coye) is green on the earlier printing, red on the later. The books are otherwise identical. Contents: *At the Mountains of Madness/The Case of Charles Dexter Ward/The Dream-Quest of Unknown Kadath/The Shunned House/The Dreams in the Witch-House/The Statement of Randolph Carter/The Silver Key/Through the Gates of the Silver Key.*

AT THE MOUNTAINS OF MADNESS: (**At the Mountains of Madness 2**)—Gollancz: London, 1967, pp 448, 30s; Panther Books: London, 02596, 1968, wpps 300, 5s; Beagle: N. Y., 1971, wpps 300, 95¢. Contents: *At the Mountains of Madness/The Dreams in the Witch-House/The Statement of Randolph Carter/The Dream-Quest of Unknown Kadath/The Silver Key/Through the Gates of the Silver Key.*

BEST SUPERNATURAL STORIES OF H. P. LOVECRAFT: (**Best Supernatural Stories**)—World Publishing Co. Cleveland, 1945, pp 307. At least 3 printings. Mainly printed on paper cheaper than that used for most pulps and sold at 49¢, but some copies of the first printing were on better paper and sold at $1.00. Some copies (at 49¢) are on both types of paper. Contents: *In the Vault/Pickman's Model/The Rats in the Walls/The Outsider/The Colour Out of Space/The Music of Erich Zann/The Haunter of the Dark/The Picture in the House/*

The Call of Cthulhu/The Dunwich Horror/Cool Air/The Whisperer in Darkness/The Terrible Old Man/The Thing on the Doorstep.

BEYOND THE WALL OF SLEEP: (**Beyond the Wall of Sleep**)—Arkham House: Sauk City, 1943, pp xxiv + 459, $5.00, 1217 copies printed. Contents: *By Way of Introduction*, by August Derleth and Donald Wandrei/*Autobiography: Some Notes on a Nonentity/The Commonplace Book/History and Chronology of the Necronomicon/Memory/What the Moon Brings/Nyarlathotep/Ex Oblivione/The Tree/The Other Gods/The Quest of Iranon/The Doom That Came to Sarnath/The White Ship/From Beyond/Beyond the Wall of Sleep/The Unnameable/The Hound/The Moon-Bog/The Evil Clergyman/Herbert West—Reanimator/The Dream-Quest of Unknown Kadath/The Case of Charles Dexter Ward/The Crawling Chaos*, with Elizabeth Berkeley/*The Green Meadow*, with Elizabeth Berkeley/*The Curse of Yig*, by Zealia Brown Reed Bishop/*The Horror in the Museum*, by Hazel Heald/*Out of the Eons*, by Hazel Heald/*The Mound*, by Zealia Brown Reed Bishop/*The Diary of Alonzo Typer*, by William Lumley/*The Challenge from Beyond*, with C. L. Moore, Frank Belknap Long, Jr., A. Merritt, and Robert E. Howard/*In the Walls of Eryx*, with Kenneth Sterling/*Ibid/Sweet Ermengarde/Providence/On a Grecian Colonnade in a Park/Old Christmas/New England Fallen/On a New England Village Seen by Moonlight/Astrophobos/Sunset/A Year Off/A Summer Sunset and Evening/To Mistress Sophia Simple, Queen of the Cinema/The Ancient Track/The Eidolon/The*

Nightmare Lake/The Outpost/The Rutted Road/ The Wood/Hallowe'en in a Suburb/Primavera/ October/To a Dreamer/Despair/Nemesis/Psychopompos/The Book/Pursuit/The Key/Recognition/ Homecoming/The Lamp/Zaman's Hill/The Port/ The Courtyard/The Pigeon-Flyers/The Well/The Howler/Hesperia/Star-Winds/Antarktos/The Window/A Memory/The Gardens of Yin/The Bells/ Night-Gaunts/Nyarlathotep/Azathoth/Mirage/The Canal/St. Toad's/The Familiar/The Elder Pharos/Expectancy/Nostalgia/Background/The Dweller/Alienation/Harbour Whistles/Recapture/Evening Star/Continuity/Yule Horror/To Mr. Finlay, Upon His Drawing for Mr. Bloch's Tale.The Faceless God/To Clark Ashton Smith, Esq., Upon His Phantastic Tales, Verse, Pictures, and Sculptures/ Where Once Poe Walked/Christmas Greetings to Mrs. Phillips Gamwell! 1925/Brick Row/The Messenger/The Cthulhu Mythos: A Glossary, by Francis Towner Laney/An Appreciation of H. P. Lovecraft, by W. Paul Cook.

COLLECTED POEMS: (Collected Poems)—Arkham House: Sauk City, 1964, pp 134, $4.00, 2013 copies printed; Ballantine: N. Y., 02147, 1971, wpps 134, 95¢ (as Fungi From Yuggoth and Other Poems). Illustrated and (in the hardcover edition) with a dust jacket by Frank Utpatel. The paperback cover is by Gervasio Gallardo. Contents: Foreword, by August Derleth/Providence/On a Grecian Colonnade in a Park/Brick Row/Old Christmas/New England Fallen/On a New England Village Seen by Moonlight/Astrophobos/Sunset/ To Pan/A Summer Sunset and Evening/To Mistress Sophia Simple, Queen of the Cinema/A Year Off/ Sir Thomas Tryout/Phaeton/August/Death/To the American Flag/To a Youth/My Favorite Character/ To Templeton and Mount Monadnock/The Poe-et's Nightmare/Lament for the Vanished Spider/Regnar Lodbrug's Epicedium/Little Sam Perkins/Drinking Song from The Tomb/The Ancient Track/The Eidolon/The Nightmare Lake/The Outpost/The Rutted Road/The Wood/The House/The City/ Hallowe'en in a Suburb/Primavera/October/To a Dreamer/Despair/Nemesis/Yule Horror/To Mr. Finlay, Upon His Drawing for Mr. Bloch's Tale, The Faceless God/Where Once Poe Walked/Christmas Greetings to Mrs. Phillips Gamwell—1925/ The Messenger/To Klarkash-Ton, Lord of Averoigne/Psychopompos/The Book/Pursuit/The Key/Recognition/Homecoming/The Lamp/Zaman's

Hill/The Port/The Courtyard/The Pigeon-Flyers/ The Well/The Howler/Hesperia/Star-Winds/Antarktos/The Window/A Memory/The Gardens of Yin/The Bells/Night-Gaunts/Nyarlathotep/Azathoth/Mirage/The Canal/St. Toad's/The Familiar/ The Elder Pharos/Expectancy/Nostalgia/Background/The Dweller/Alienation/Harbour Whistles/ Recapture/Evening Star/Continuity.

THE COLOUR OUT OF SPACE: (The Colour Out of Space)—Lancer Books: N. Y., 73-425, 1964, wpps 222, 50¢; 73-608, 1967, 74-501, 1969; 75-248, 1971, 95¢. Contents: In the Vault/The Outsider/The Colour Out of Space/The Picture in the House/ The Call of Cthulhu/Cool Air/The Whisperer in Darkness/The Terrible Old Man.

CRY HORROR: see THE LURKING FEAR 1 . . . .

DAGON AND OTHER MACABRE TALES: (Dagon 1)— Arkham House: Sauk City, 1965, pp 424, $6.50, 3471 copies printed; Gollancz: London, 1967, pp 424, 30s. Jacket of the U. S. edition is by Lee Brown Coye; jacket of the British is the usual Gollancz. Contents: Introduction, by August Derleth/Dagon/The Tomb/Polaris/Beyond the Wall of Sleep/The Doom That Came to Sarnath/The White Ship/Arthur Jermyn/The Cats of Ulthar/ Celephais/From Beyond/The Temple/The Tree/ The Moon-Bog/The Nameless City/The Other Gods/The Quest of Iranon/Herbert West—Reanimator/The Hound/Hypnos/The Lurking Fear/The Festival/The Unnameable/Imprisoned with the Pharaohs/He/The Horror at Red Hook/The Strange High House in the Mist/In the Walls of Eryx, with Kenneth Sterling/The Evil Clergyman/The Beast in the Cave/The Alchemist/Poetry and the Gods, with Anna Helen Crofts/The Street/The Transition of Juan Romero/Azathoth/The Descendant/ The Book/The Thing in the Moonlight/Supernatural Horror in Literature.

DAGON AND OTHER TALES: (Dagon 2)—Panther Books, London 1969m wpps 223, 6s; Beagle: N. Y.,   , 1971, wpps 223, 95¢. Contents: Dagon/Polaris/ Beyond the Wall of Sleep/The Doom that Came to Sarnath/The White Ship/The Cats of Ulthar/ Celephais/From Beyond/The Temple/The Tree/ The Other Gods/The Quest of Iranon/Herbert West—Reanimator/Hypnos/Supernatural Horror in Literature.

THE DARK BROTHERHOOD AND OTHER PIECES: (The Dark Brotherhood)—Arkham House:S auk City, 1966, pp 321, $5.00, 3500 copies printed. Dust jacket by Frank Utpatel. Contents: *Introduction*, by August Derleth/*The Dark Brotherhood*, with August Derleth/*Suggestions for a Reading Guide/ Alfredo/Amateur Journalism: Its Possible Needs and Betterment/What Belongs in Verse/Bells/ Oceanus/Clouds/Mother Earth/Cindy/On a Battlefield in France/Deaf, Dumb, and Blind*, by C. M. Eddy, Jr./*The Ghost Eater*, by C. M. Eddy, Jr./*The Loved Dead*, by C. M. Eddy, Jr./*The Lovecraft "Books": Some Addenda and Corrigenda*, by William Scott Home/*To Arkham and the Stars*, by Fritz Leiber/*Through Hyperspace with Brown Jenkin*, by Fritz Leiber/*Lovecraft and the New England Megaliths*, by Andrew E. Rothovius/ *H. P. L.: A Bibliography*, by Jack L. Chalker/ *Walks With Lovecraft*, by C. M. Eddy, Jr./*The Cancer of Superstition*, with C. M. Eddy, Jr./*The Making of a Hoax*, by August Derleth/*Lovecraft's Illustrators*, by John E. Vetter/*Final Notes*, by August Derleth.

THE DREAM-QUEST OF UNKNOWN KADATH: (**The Dream-Quest of Unknown Kadath**)—Ballantine: N. Y., 01923 1923, 1970, wpps 242, 95¢. Contents: *The Dream-Quest of Unknown Kadath/Celephais/The Silver Key/Through the Gates of the Silver Key/The White Ship/The Strange High House in the Mist.*

DREAMS AND FANCIES: (**Dreams and Fancies**)—Arkham House: Sauk City, 1962, pp 174, $3.50, 2030 copies printed, dust jacket by R. Taylor. Contents: *Introduction*, by August Derleth/*Excerpts from letters/Night-Gaunts/Memory/The Statement of Randolph Carter/Celephais/The Doom that Came to Sarnath/Nyarlathotep/The Evil Clergyman/The Thing in the Moonlight/The Shadow Out of Time.*

THE DUNWICH HORROR: (**The Dunwich Horror 1**)—Bartholomew House: N. Y., 1945, pp 186, 25¢. Contents: *The Dunwich Horror/The Thing on the Doorstep/The Shadow Out of Time.*

THE DUNWICH HORROR AND OTHER WEIRD TALES: (**The Dunwich Horror 2**)—Armed Services Editions, #730, 1945, wpps 384. Contents: *Introduction*, by August Derleth/*The Dunwich Horror/In the Vault/ The Rats in the Walls/Pickman's Model/The Music of Erich Zann/The Colour Out of Space/ The Outsider/The Call of Cthulhu/The Whisperer in Darkness/The Shadow Over Innsmouth/The Moon-Bog/The Hound.*

THE DUNWICH HORROR AND OTHERS: THE BEST SUPERNATURAL STORIES OF H. P. LOVECRAFT: (**The Dunwich Horror 3**)—Arkham House: Sauk City, 1963, pp xx + 421, $5.00; 1966, $6.50; 1971, $7.50. First printing is of 3133 copies, second and third of 3000 copies each. Second printing has an extra gold band on the spine, otherwise it is identical to the first; third printing is identified as a reprint. Dust jacket by Lee Brown Coye. Contents: *H. P. Lovecraft and His Work*, by August Derleth/*In the Vault/Pickman's Model/ The Rats in the Walls/The Outsider/The Colour Out of Space/The Music of Erich Zann/The Haunter of the Dark/The Picture in the House/ The Call of Cthulhu/The Dunwich Horror/Cool Air/The Whisperer in Darkness/The Terrible Old Man/The Thing on the Doorstep/The Shadow Over Innsmouth/The Shadow Out of Time.*

THE DUNWICH HORROR AND OTHERS: (**The Dunwich Horror 4**)—Lancer: N. Y., 72-702, 1963, wpps 158, 50¢ (1967, 60¢; 1971, 95¢). Contents: *H. P. Lovecraft and His Work*, by August Derleth/*Pickman's Model/The Rats in the Walls/The Music of Erich Zann/The Haunter of the Dark/The Dunwich Horror/The Thing on the Doorstep.*

FUNGI FROM YUGGOTH: (**Fungi From Yuggoth**)—William H. Evans: Eugene, Oregon, 1943, wpps 38, mimeographed, less than 100 copies done. Contents: *The Book/Pursuit/The Key/Recognition/Homecoming/The Lamp/Zaman's Hill/The Port/The Courtyard/The Pigeon-Flyers/The Well/ The Howler/Hesperia/Star-Winds/Antarktos/The Window/A Memory/The Gardens of Yin/The Bells/ Night-Gaunts/Nyarlathotep/Azathoth/Mirage/The Canal/St. Toad's/The Familiars/The Elder Pharos/Expectancy/Nostalgia/Background/TheDweller/Alienation/Harbour Whistles.* This first collection is three short (*Recapture/Evening Star/ Continuity*) of the full set.

FUNGI FROM YUGGOTH AND OTHER POEMS: *see* Collected Poems. . . .

H. P. L.: (**H. P. L.**)—Corwin Stickney: N. J., 1937, wpps 16, 25 copies printed by letterpress. Contents: *Introduction* (unsigned, but by Stickney)/ *The Wood/Homecoming/Nostalgia/Night-Gaunts/ The Dweller/Harbour Whistles/In a Sequestered Churchyard Where Once Poe Walked/Astrophobos.*

THE HAUNTER OF THE DARK AND OTHER TALES OF HORROR: (**The Haunter of the Dark**)—Victor Gollancz: London, 1951, pp 303, 12/6; 1966, 25s. Contents: *Introduction*, by August Derleth/*The Outsider/The Dunwich Horror/The Rats in the*

Walls/The Call of Cthulhu/Pickman's Model/The Whisperer in Darkness/The Colour Out of Space/ The Music of Erich Zann/The Haunter of the Dark/ The Thing on the Doorstep.

THE HORROR IN THE MUSEUM AND OTHER REVISIONS: **(The Horror in the Museum)**—Arkham House: Sauk City, 1970, pp 383, $7.50, 4000 copies printed; Beagle: N. Y., 95159, 1971, wpps 245, 95¢. Hardcover dust jacket is by Gahan Wilson. All stories are revised by Lovecraft. Contents: *Lovecraft's "Revisions,"* by August Derleth/*The Crawling Chaos*, with Elizabeth Berkeley/*The Green Meadow*, with Elizabeth Berkeley/*The Invisible Monster*, by Sonia Greene/*Four O'Clock*, by Sonia Greene/*The Man of Stone*, by Hazel Heald/*Winged Death*, by Hazel Heald/*The Loved Dead*, by C. M. Eddy, Jr./*Deaf, Dumb, and Blind*, by C. M. Eddy, Jr./*The Ghost-Eater*, by C. M. Eddy, Jr./*"Till All the Seas,"* by Robert H. Barlow/*The Horror in the Museum*, by Hazel Heald/ *Out of the Eons*, by Hazel Heald/*The Diary of Alonzo Typer*, by William Lumley/*The Horror in the Burying Ground*, by Hazel Heald/*The Last Test*, by Adolphe de Castro/*The Electric Executioner*, by Adolphe de Castro/*The Curse of Yig*, by Zealia Brown Reed Bishop/*The Mound*, by Zealia Brown Reed Bishop/*Two Black Bottles*, by Wilfred Blanch Talman.

THE LOVECRAFT COLLECTOR'S LIBRARY: **(LCL)**—ed. George T. Wetzel—SSR Publications: Tonawanda, N. Y. 75 numbered copies per volume. Mimeographed.

VOLUME I: SELECTED ESSAYS: **(LCL, Vol. I)**— 1952. 26 pages. Contents: *Poetry and the Gods/ Idealism and Materialism/A Confession of Unfaith/Nietzscheism and Realism.*

VOLUME II: SELECTED ESSAYS II: **(LCL, Vol. II)**— 1952. 25 pages. Contents: *The Street/A Descent to Avernus/The Brief Autobiography of an Inconsequential Scribbler/Anglo-Saxondom/Revolutionary Mythology/The Trip of Theobald/The Alchemist.*

VOLUME III: SELECTED POETRY: **(LCL, Vol. III)**— 1953. 28 pages. Contents: *The Bells/The Voice/ On the Death of a Rhyming Critic/Monos: An Ode/Inspiration/Hylas and Myrrha, A Tale/ Ambition/The Bookstall/On Receiving a Picture of Swans/To Edward Plunkett, Baron Dunsany/ To Mr. Lockhart, on His Poetry/Autumn/Interum Conjunctae/To the Eighth of November/The Pensive Swain.*

VOLUME IV: SELECTED POETRY II: **(LCL, Vol. IV)**—1955. 32 pages. Contents: *Oceanus/Clouds/ Mother Earth/Vers Rusticum/Earth and Sky/Prologue/Solstice/The Garden/Nathicana/The Poet of Passion/Lines for the Poet's Night at the Scribbler's Club/Cindy: Scrub Lady in a State Street Skyscraper/The Dead Bookworm/Ave Atque Vale/The Dream/Ye Ballade of Patrick von Flynn/ Pacifist's War Song/The Nymph's Reply to the Modern Business Man/Grace* (and *Ward Phillips Replies)/To Greece, 1917/Lines on the 25th Anniversary of the* Providence Evening News/ *Fact and Fancy.*

VOLUME V: THE AMATEUR JOURNALIST: **(LCL, Vol. V)**—1955. 33 pages. Contents: *The Simple Spelling Mania/The President's Message/Amateur Criticism/The Symphonic Ideal/The Professional Incubus/A Reply to the Lingerer/ Concerning "Persia—In Europe"/Les Mouches Fantastiques/Looking Backward.*

THE LURKING FEAR AND OTHER STORIES: **(The Lurking Fear 1)**—Avon Book Company: N. Y., 1947, wpps 223, 25¢; as **Cry Horror!**, Avon Books: N. Y., 1958, wpps 223, 35¢; as **Cry Horror!**, World Distributors Ltd.; London & Manchester, 1959, wpps 223, ³⁄₆. The third printing is from the same plates as the second; the first is from different plates, despite having the same page count. Contents: *The Lurking Fear/The Colour Out of Space/ The Nameless City/Pickman's Model/Arthur Jermyn/The Shunned House/The Hound/Cool Air/ The Moon-Bog/The Unnamable/The Call of Cthulhu.*

THE LURKING FEAR AND OTHER STORIES: **(The Lurking Fear 2)**—Panther Books: London, 1964, wpps 208, ²⁄₆; Beagle Books: N. Y., 95042, 1970, wpps 182, 95¢. Contents: *In the Vault/The Picture in the House/Cool Air/The Terrible Old Man/The Shadow Over Innsmouth/The Shadow Out of Time/The Lurking Fear/The Nameless City/Arthur Jermyn/ The Unnamable/The Moon-Bog/The Hound/The Shunned House.*

MARGINALIA: **(Marginalia)**—Arkham House: Sauk City, 1944, pp 377, $3.00. 2035 copies printed; dust jacket by Virgil Finlay. Contents: *Foreword*, by August Derleth and Donald Wandrei/*Imprisoned with the Pharaohs*, by Houdini/*Medusa's Coil*, by Zealia Brown Reed Bishop/*Winged Death*, by Hazel Heald/*The Man of Stone*, by Hazel Heald/ *Notes on the Writing of Weird Fiction/Some Notes* on *Interplanetary Fiction/Lord Dunsany and His Work/Heritage or Modernism: Common Sense in Art Forms/Some Backgrounds of Fairyland/Some Causes of Self-Immolation/A Guide to Charleston, South Carolina/Observations on Several Parts of North America/The Beast in the Cave/The Transition of Juan Romero/Azathoth/The Book/The Descendant/The Very Old Folk/The Thing in the Moonlight/Two Comments/H. P. Lovecraft: An Appreciation*, by Thomas Ollive Mabbot/*His Own Most Fantastic Creation*, by Winfield Townley Scott/*Some Random Memories of H. P. L.*, by Frank Belknap Long/*H. P. Lovecraft in Florida*, by Robert H. Barlow/*Lovecraft and Science*, by Kenneth Sterling/*Lovecraft as a Formative Influence*, by August Derleth/*The Dweller in Darkness*, by Donald Wandrei/*H. P. Lovecraft*, by Frank Belknap Long/*To Howard Phillips Lovecraft*, by Clark Ashton Smith/*H. P. L.*, by Henry Kuttner/*Lost Dream*, by Emil Petaja/*To Howard Phillips Lovecraft*, by Francis Flagg/*Elegy: In Providence in the Spring*, by August Derleth/*The Outsider: H. P. Lovecraft*, by Charles E. White/*In Memory: H. P. Lovecraft*, by Richard Ely Morse.

THE OUTSIDER AND OTHERS: (**The Outsider**)—Arkham House: Sauk City, 1939, pp 553, $5.00. 1258 copies printed, jacket by Virgil Finlay. Contents: *Howard Phillips Lovecraft: Outsider*, by August Derleth and Donald Wandrei/*Dagon/Polaris/Celephais/Hypnos/The Cats of Ulthar/The Strange High House in the Mist/The Statement of Randolph Carter/The Silver Key/Through the Gates of the Silver Key/The Outsider/The Music of Erich Zann/The Rats in the Walls/Cool Air/He/The Horror at Red Hook/The Temple/Arthur Jermyn/The Picture in the House/The Festival/The Terrible Old Man/The Tomb/The Shunned House/In the Vault/Pickman's Model/The Haunter of the Dark/The Dreams in the Witch-House/The Thing on the Doorstep/The Nameless City/The Lurking Fear/The Call of Cthulhu/The Colour Out of Space/The Dunwich Horror/The Whisperer in Darkness/The Shadow Over Innsmouth/The Shadow Out of Time/At the Mountains of Madness/Supernatural Horror in Literature.*

SELECTED LETTERS: I (1911-1924)—Arkham House: Sauk City, 1965, pp 362, $7.50. 2504 copies printed; jacket by Gary Gore and Virgil Finlay.

SELECTED LETTERS: II (1925-1929)—Arkham House: Sauk City, 1968, pp 359, $7.50. 3500 copies printed; jacket by Gary Gore and Virgil Finlay.

SELECTED LETTERS: III (1929-1931)—Arkham House: Sauk City, 1971, pp 451, $10.00. 2500 copies printed; jacket by Gary Gore and Virgil Finlay.

THE SHADOW OUT OF TIME AND OTHER TALES OF HORROR: (**The Shadow Out of Time**)—Victor Gollancz: London, 1968, pp 384, 35s. Contents: *In the Vault/The Picture in the House/Cool Air/The Terrible Old Man/The Shadow Out of Time/The Shadow Over Innsmouth/The Survivor/Wentworth's Day/The Peabody Heritage/The Gable Window/The Ancestor/The Shadow Out of Space/The Lamp of Alhazred/The Fisherman of Falcon Point/The Dark Brotherhood/The Shuttered Room.* The last ten of these are in collaboration with August Derleth.

THE SHUTTERED ROOM AND OTHER PIECES: (**The Shuttered Room 1**)—Arkham House: Sauk City, 1959, pp 313, $5.00. 2500 copies printed; jacket by R. Taylor. Contents: *Foreword*, by August Derleth/*The Shuttered Room* (with August Derleth)/*The Fisherman of Falcon Point* (with August Derleth)/*The Little Glass Bottle/The Secret Cave/The Mystery of the Graveyard/The Mysterious Ship/The Alchemist/Poetry and the Gods/The Street/Old Bugs/Idealism and Materialism: A Reflection/The Commonplace Book* (annotated by August Derleth)/*Lovecraft in Providence*, by Donald Wandrei/*Lovecraft as Mentor*, by August Derleth/*Out of the Ivory Tower*, by Robert Bloch/*Three Hours with H. P. Lovecraft*, by Dorothy C. Walker/*Memories of a Friendship*, by Alfred Galpin/*Homage to H. P. L.*, by Felix Stefanile/*H. P. L.*, by Clark Ashton Smith/*Lines to H. P. Lovecraft*, by Joseph Payne Brennan/*Revenants*, by August Derleth/*The Barlow Tributes/H. P. Lovecraft: The Books*, by Lin Carter/*H. P. Lovecraft: The Gods*, by Lin Carter/*Addendum: Some Observations on the Carter Glossary*, by T. G. L. Cockcroft/*Notes on the Cthulhu Mythos*, by George T. Wetzel/*Lovecraft's First Book*, by William L. Crawford/*Dagon/The Strange High House in the Mist/The Outsider.*

THE SHUTTERED ROOM AND OTHER TALES OF HORROR: (**The Shuttered Room 2**)—Panther Books: London, 1970, wpps 205, 30p. Contents: *The Survivor/Wentworth's Day/The Peabody Heritage/The Gable Window/The Ancestor/The Shadow Out of Space/The Lamp of Alhazred/The Fisherman of Falcon Point/The Dark Brotherhood/The Shuttered Room.*

THE SHUTTERED ROOM AND OTHER STORIES: (**The Shuttered Room 3**)—Beagle: N. Y., 95068, 1971, wpps 166, 95¢. Contents: *The Shuttered Room/ The Fisherman of Falcon Point/The Dark Brotherhood/Witch's Hollow/The Shadow in the Attic/ The Horror from the Middle Span.*

SOMETHING ABOUT CATS AND OTHER PIECES: (**Something About Cats**)—Arkham House: Sauk City, 1949, pp 309, $3.00. 2995 copies printed; jacket by Ronald Clyne. Contents: *Prefatory Note*, by August Derleth/*Something About Cats/The Invisible Monster*, by Sonia H. Greene/*Four O'Clock*, by Sonia H. Greene/*The Horror in the Burying Ground*, by Hazel Heald/*The Last Test*, by Adolph de Castro/*The Electric Executioner*, by Adolph de Castro/*Satan's Servants*, by Robert Bloch/*The Despised Pastoral/Time and Space/Merlinus Redivivus/At the Root/The Materialist Today/ Vermont: A First Impression/The Battle That Ended the Century/Notes for "The Shadow Over Innsmouth"/Discarded Draft for "The Shadow Over Innsmouth"/Notes for "At the Mountains of Madness"/Notes for "The Shadow Out of Time"/ Phaeton/August/Death/To the American Flag/To A Youth/My Favorite Character/To Templeton and Mount Monadnock/The House/The City/The Poe-et's Nightmare/Sir Thomas Tryout/Lament for the Vanished Spider/Regnar Lodbrug's Epicedium/A Memoir of Lovecraft*, by Rheinhart Kleiner/*Howard Phillips Lovecraft*, by Samuel Loveman/*Lovecraft as I Knew Him*, by Sonia Davis/*Addenda to* H. P. L.: A Memoir, by August Derleth (*Lovecraft's Sensitivity/Lovecraft's Conservative*)/*The Man Who Was Lovecraft*, by E. Hoffman Price/*A Literary Copernicus*, by Fritz Leiber/*H. P. L.*, by Vincent Starrett/*Providence: Two Gentlemen Meet at Midnight*, by August Derleth.

THE SURVIVOR AND OTHERS: (**The Survivor**)—Arkham House: Sauk City, 1957, pp 161, $3.00. 2096 copies printed, jacket by Ronald Chyne. Ballantine: N. Y., 629, 1962, wpps 143, 35¢ (02148, 1971, 95¢). Contents: *The Survivor/Wentworth's Day/The Peabody Heritage/The Gable Window/ The Ancestor/The Shadow Out of Space/The Lamp of Alhazred.*

THREE TALES OF HORROR: (**Three Tales of Horror**)—Arkham House: Sauk City, 1967, pp 135, $7.50. 1000 copies printed, jacket and illustrations by Lee Brown Coye. Contents: *Introduction*, by August Derleth/*The Colour Out of Space/The Thing on the Doorstep/The Dunwich Horror.*

THE TOMB: (**The Tomb**)—Panther Books: London, 02903, 1969, wpps 190, 5s; Beagle: N. Y., 95032, 1971, wpps 190, 95¢. Contents: *The Tomb/The Festival/Imprisoned With the Pharaohs/He/The Horror at Red Hook/The Strange High House in the Mist/In the Walls of Eryx/The Evil Clergyman/ The Beast in the Cave/The Alchemist/Poetry and the Gods/The Street/The Thing in the Moonlight/ The Transition of Juan Romero/Azathoth/The Descendant/The Book*

THE WEIRD SHADOW OVER INNSMOUTH AND OTHER STORIES OF THE SUPERNATURAL: (**The Weird Shadow Over Innsmouth**)—Bartholomew House: N. Y., 1944, wpps 190, 25¢. Contents: *The Shadow Over Innsmouth/The Outsider/He/The Festival/The Whisperer in Darkness.*

Foreign - language

FRENCH

LA COULEUR TOMBEÉ DU CIEL: Editions Denoël: Paris, 1954, wpps 239. Contents: *La Couleur Tombeé du Ciel/L'Abomination de Dunwich/La Cauchemar d'Innsmouth/Celui qui Chuchotait dans les Tenebres*. Translated by Jacques Papy, with an introduction by Jacques Bergier. (*The Colour Out of Space/The Dunwich Horror/The Shadow Over Innsmouth/The Whisperer in Darkness*).

DANS L'ABIME DU TEMPS: Editions Denoël: Paris, 1954, wpps 244. Contents: *Dans l'Abime du Temps/La Maison de la Sorciere/L'Appel de Cthulhu/Les Montagnes Hallucinees*. Translated by Jacques Papy. (*The Shadow Out of Time/Dreams in the Witch-House/The Call of Cthulhu/At the Mountains of Madness*).

DEMONS ET MERVEILLES: (1)–Deux-Rives: Paris, 1955, wpps 203. Contents: *Le Temoignage de Randolph Carter/La Clé d'Argent/A Travers les Portes de la Clé d'Argent/A la Recherche de Kadath*. Translated by Bernard Noël. (*The Statement of Randolph Carter/The Silver Key/Through the Gates of the Silver Key/The Dream-Quest of Unknown Kadath–i. e.*, the Randolph Carter stories).

DEMONS ET MERVEILLES: (2)–Editions le Bibliotheque Moniale: Paris, nd (1955?), pp 178. Contents: *A Travers les Portes de la Clé d'Argent/A la Recherche de Kadath*. Translated by Bernard Noel, with an introduction by Jacques Bergier. (*Through the Gates of the Silver Key/The Dream-Quest of Unknown Kadath*).

JE SUIS D'AILLEURS: Editions Denoël: Paris, 1961, wpps 216. Contents: *Je suis d'Ailleurs/La Musique d'Erich Zann/L'Indicible/Air Froid/Le Molosse/La Maison Maudité/Le Tourbiere Hanteé/Arthur Jermyn/Le Modele de Pickman/La Cité sans Nom/La Peur que Rode*. Translated by Yves Riviere. (*The Outsider/The Music of Erich Zann/The Unnamable/Cool Air/The Hound/The Shunned House/The Moon-Bog/The Nameless City/The Lurking Fear*.

PAR DÉLÀ LE MUR DU SOMMIEL: Editions Denoël: Paris, 1956, wpps 237. Contents: *Par délà le Mur du Sommiel/Les Rats dans les Murs/Le Monstre sur le Seuil/Celui qui Hantait les Tenebres/L'Affaire Charles Dexter Ward*. Translated by Jacques Papy. (*Beyond the Wall of Sleep/The Rats in the Walls/The Thing on the Doorstep/The Haunter of the Dark/The Case of Charles Dexter Ward*.

There is also DAGON ET AUTRES RÉCITS DE TERREUR: Belfond: Paris, 1970, pp 349, 26F. Translated by Paule Pérez, with a preface by Francois Truchaud, about which no collection information is available, save that there were only 21 untranslated stories, mostly forgettable.

SPANISH

EN COLO QUE CAYO DEL CIELO: Ediciones Minotauro: Buenos Aires, 1957, wpps 315. Contents: *El Llamado de Cthulhu/El Color que Cayo del Cielo/El que Susurraba en las Tinieblas/En las Montañas Alucinantes*. Translated and with an introduction by Ricardo Gosseyn. (*The Call of Cthulhu/The Colour Out of Space/The Whisperer in Darkness/At the Mountains of Madness*).

There is also EN LAS MONTANAS DE LA LOCURA: Seix y Barral: Barcelona, 1968, pp 175. Translated by Calvert Casey, for which no contents are available.

JAPANESE

DUNWICH NO KAI: Tôkyô Sôgensha: Tokyo, 1969, wpps 403, translated by Hashimoto Fukuo and Onishi Tadaaki, for which no contents are available.

GERMAN

BERGE DES WAHNSINNS (Zwei Horrorgeschichten): Insel Verlag: Frankfurt, 1970, pp 224, DM 14.50. Contents: *Berge des Wahnsinns/Der Flüsterer im Dunkeln*. In the series **Bibliothek des Hauses Usher**, ed. Kalju Kirde. Translated by Rudolf Hermstein, jacket by Osterwalder. (*At the Mountains of Madness/The Whisperer in Darkness*).

CTHULHU (Geistergeschichten von H. P. Lovecraft): Insel Verlag: Frankfurt, 1968, pp 239, DM 4.80. Suhrkamp Verlag: Frankfurt, 1972, wpps 239, DM 4.00. Contents: *Pickman's Modell/Die Ratten im Gemäuer/Die Musik des Erich Zann/Der leuchtende Trapezoeder/Das Grauen von Dunwich/Cthulhus Ruf*. Translated by Hans Carl Artmann, introduction by Giorgio Manganelli. Jacket by Heinz Edelmann (hardback); by Hans Ulrich and Ute Osterwalder (paperback). (*Pickman's Model/The Rats in the Walls/The Music of Erich Zann/The Haunter of the Dark/The Dunwich Horror/The Call of Cthulhu.*

DAS DING AUF DER SCHWELLE (Unheimliche Geschichten): Insel Verlag: Frankfurt, 1969, pp 214, DM 12.50, 6000 copy edition. Contents: *Das Ding auf der Schwelle/Der Außenseiter/Die Farbe aus dem All/Träume im Hexenhaus/Der Schatten aus der Zeit*. In the series **Bibliothek des Hauses Usher**, ed. Kalju Kirde. Translated by Rudolf Hermstein, jacket by Hans Ulrich and Ute Osterwalder. (*The Thing on the Threshold/The Outsider/The Colour Out of Space/Dreams in the Witch House/The Shadow Out of Time*).

DER FALL CHARLES DEXTER WARD (Zwei Horrorgeschichten): Insel Verlag: Frankfurt, 1971, pp 251, DM 14.50. Contents: *Der Fall Charles Dexter Ward/Schatten über Innsmouth*. In the series **Bibliothek des Hauses Usher**, ed. Kalju Kirde. Translated by Rudolf Hermstein, jacket by H. U. Osterwalder. (*The Case of Charles Dexter Ward/The Shadow Over Innsmouth.*

TRÄUME IM HEXENHAUS: Anabis Verlag: Berlin, 1971, pp 46, DM 12.80. Contents: *Träume im Hexenhaus*. In the series **Sammlung Anabis**, ed. Holger Hartwig and Roland Kloss. Translated by Joachim A. Frank. Illustrated by Peter Collien. (*The Dreams in the Witch-House*).

ZWÖLF GRUSEL STORIES: Wilhelm Heyne Verlag: München, 1961, wpps 302, DM 4.80. Contents: *H. P. Lovecraft und sein Werk*, von August Derleth/*In der Gruft/Pickmans Modell/Die Farbe aus dem All/Das dunkle Alptraum/Das Bild in dem Haus/Der Schrecken von Dunwich/Kühle Luft/Das Flüstern in Dunkeln/Der Schreckliche Alte/Das Ding auf der Schwelle/Der Schatten über Innsmouth/Der Aussenseiter*. Translated by Wulf H. Bergner (*In the Vault/Pickman's Model/The Colour Out of Space/The Shadow Out of Time/The Picture in the House/The Dunwich Horror/Cool Air/The Whisperer in Darkness/The Terrible Old Man/The Thing on the Doorstep/The Shadow Over Innsmouth/The Outsider*).

NOTE: Except for **12 Grusel Stories**, information on the German entries was received too late for cross-referencing in the other chapters.

DUTCH

HET GEFUISTER IN DE DUISTERNIS: Brunau: Vitgevers, 1968, wpps 189, 40Bf. Contents: *In the Maelstrom of Azathoth*, by Aart C. Prins/*De Vizioenen van Richard Pickman/De Lokroep van Cthulhu/De Muziek van Erich Zann/De Buitenstaander/Het Gefluister in de Duisternis*. (*Pickman's Model/The Call of Cthulhu/The Music of Erich Zann/The Outsider/The Whisperer in Darkness*.

MAKABERE VERHALEN: Uitgeverij Contact: Amsterdam, 1967, pp 118, 115Bf. Contents: *De Kleur Vit de Ruimte/De Bezoer Vit De Duisternis/Dagon/Het Omzienbare/Hij/De Tempel*. Translated by Jean A. Schalekamp. (*The Colour Out of Space/The Haunter of the Dark/Dagon/From Beyond/He/The Temple*).

CHAPTER 5

Revisions

THE FOLLOWING stories are listed in the chapter on Mythos Stories to avoid repetition: "The Curse of Yig," "Medusa's Coil," and "The Mound," by Zealia Brown Reed Bishop, "The Horror in the Museum," and "Out of the Eons" by Hazel Heald, and "The Diary of Alonzo Typer" by William Lumley.

ROBERT H. BARLOW

"TILL ALL THE SEAS": *The Californian*,   , 1935; *The Arkham Collector* #4, Winter 1969; in The Horror in the Museum (q. v.).

ROBERT BLOCH

SATAN'S SERVANTS: original in Something About Cats (q. v.); *Magazine of Horror* #30, December 1969.

ADOLPHE de CASTRO

THE ELECTRIC EXECUTIONER: *Weird Tales*, August 1930; in Something About Cats (q. v.); in The Horror in the Museum (q. v.).

THE LAST TEST: *Weird Tales*, November 1928; in Something About Cats (q. v.); in The Horror in the Museum (q. v.).

SONIA H. GREENE DAVIS

FOUR O'CLOCK: in Something About Cats (q. v.); in The Horror in the Museum (q. v.).

THE INVISIBLE MONSTER: *Weird Tales*, November 1923; in Something About Cats (q. v.); in The Horror in the Museum (q. v.).

CLIFFORD M. EDDY, Jr.

DEAF, DUMB, AND BLIND: *Weird Tales*, April 1925; included in The Sleeping and the Dead, ed. August Derleth (Pellegrini & Cudahy: N. Y., 1947, pp 518, $3.75); in The Dark Brotherhood (q. v.); in The Horror in the Museum (q. v.).

THE GHOST-EATER: *Weird Tales*, April 1924, included in Shapes of the Supernatural, ed. Seon Manley and Gogo Lewis (Doubleday: N. Y., 1969, pp x + 370, $5.95); in The Dark Brotherhood (q. v.).

THE LOVED DEAD: *Weird Tales*, May-June-July 1924; included in **Night's Yawning Peal**, ed. August Derleth (Pellegrini & Cudahy/Arkham House: N. Y., 1952, pp 288, $3.00); included in **The Unspeakable People**, ed. Peter Haining (Leslie Frewin: London, 1969, pp 246, 30s); (Popular Library: N. Y., 01376, 1970, wpps 207, 75¢); in **The Dark Brotherhood** (q. v.).

HAZEL HEALD

THE HORROR IN THE BURYING GROUND: *Weird Tales*, May 1937, included in **Sleep No More**, ed. August Derleth (Rinehart: N. Y., 1944, pp 374, $2.50)

(Armed Services edition, nd, np); in **Something About Cats** (q. v.); in **The Horror in the Museum** (q. v.).

THE MAN OF STONE: *Wonder Stories*, October 1932; in **Marginalia** (q. v.); in **The Horror in the Museum** (q. v.).

WINGED DEATH: *Weird Tales*, March 1934; in **Marginalia** (q. v.); in **The Horror in the Museum** (q. v.).

WILFRED BLANCH TALMAN

TWO BLACK BOTTLES: *Weird Tales*, August 1927; in **The Horror in the Museum** (q. v.).

CHAPTER 6

Mythos Stories

THIS IS unquestionably the source of more abstruse and ultimately fruitless discussions (though they are enjoyable) than any other. *Any* list is going to be somewhat personal. The following is the product of the Chalker, Berglund, Weinberg, and Carter lists, plus much mulling and muttering on my part.

AMBROSE BIERCE

AN INHABITANT OF CARCOSA: included in **The Spawn of Cthulhu** (q.v.); and many other places, including, of course, *Magazine of Horror* #14, Winter 1966.

ZEALIA BROWN REED BISHOP

THE CURSE OF YIG: *Weird Tales*, November 1929; *Weird Tales*, April 1939; *Avon Fantasy Reader* #14 (1950); in **Beyond the Wall of Sleep** (q.v.); included in **The Second Avon Fantasy Reader**, ed. George Ernsberger and Donald A. Wollheim (Avon: N.Y., 5385, 1969, wpps 173, 60¢); included in **Switch On the Light**, ed. Christine Campbell Thomson (Selwyn Blount: London, 1931, pp 256, 2s); included in **Not At Night Omnibus**, ed. Christine Campbell Thomson (Selwyn Blount: London, 1937, pp 510, ⅖); included in **Not At Night** (paper), ed. Christine Campbell Thomson (Arrow: London 586, 1960, wpps 192, ⅖); included in **The Macabre Reader**, ed. Donald A. Wollheim (Ace: N.Y., D-353, 1959, wpps 223, 35¢); (Digit: London D362, 1960, wpps 188, 2s); in **The Spawn of Cthulhu** (q.v.); in **The Curse of Yig** (Arkham House: Sauk City, 1953, pp 175, $2.50); in **The Horror in the Museum** (q.v.).

MEDUSA'S COIL: *Weird Tales*, January 1939; in **Marginalia** (q.v.); in **The Horror in the Museum** (q.v.); in **The Curse of Yig** (Arkham House: Sauk City, 1953, pp 175, $2.50).

THE MOUND: *Weird Tales*, November 1940 (abr); in **Beyond the Wall of Sleep** (q.v.); in **The Horror in The Museum** (q.v.); in **The Curse of Yig** (Arkham House: Sauk City, 1953, pp 175, $2.50).

ROBERT BLOCH

THE CREEPER IN THE CRYPT: *Weird Tales*, July 1937.

THE DARK DEMON: *Weird Tales*, November 1936; in **The Opener of the Way** (Arkham House: Sauk City, 1945, pp xi + 309, $3.00); in a later pb collection.

THE FACELESS GOD: *Weird Tales*, May 1936; *Magazine of Horror* #13, Winter 1965-66; in **The Opener of the Way** (Arkham House: Sauk City, 1945, pp xi + 309, $3.00); in a later pb collection.

THE GRINNING GHOUL: *Weird Tales*, June 1936; included in **Weird Tales of the Supernatural**, ed. Kurt Singer (W. H. Allen: London, 1966, pp 352, 30s); in **Bloch and Bradbury** (Tower: N.Y., 43-247, 1969, wpps 140, 60¢); (Peacock Press, 1972, wpps 80, $1.00).

THE MANNIKIN: *Weird Tales*, April 1937, included in **Sleep No More**, ed. August Derleth (Rinehart: N. Y., 1944, pp 374, $2.50); (Armed Services ed, nd, np); in **The Opener of the Way** (Arkham House: Sauk City, 1945, pp xi + 309, $3.00); in a later pb collection.

THE NIGHT THEY CRASHED THE PARTY: *Weird Tales*, November 1953.

NOTEBOOK FOUND IN A DESERTED HOUSE: *Weird Tales*, May 1951; included in **Tales of the Cthulhu Mythos**, ed. August Derleth (q. v.).

THE SECRET IN THE TOMB: *Weird Tales*, May 1935.

THE SHADOW FROM THE STEEPLE: *Weird Tales*, September 1950; included in **Ghost Omnibus**, ed. Kurt Singer (W. H. Allen: London, 1965, pp 287, 25s); (Four Square Books: London, 1961, 1967, wpps 126, ³⁄₆); included in **Tales of the Cthulhu Mythos**, ed. August Derleth (q. v.); in **Bloch and Bradbury** (Tower: N. Y., 43-247, 1969, wpps 140, 60¢); (Peacock Press, 1972, wpps 80, $1.00).

THE SHAMBLER FROM THE STARS: *Weird Tales*, September 1935; included in **Tales of the Cthulhu Mythos**, ed. August Derleth (q. v.); in **The Opener of the Way**; in a later pb collection.

J. RAMSEY CAMPBELL

THE CHURCH IN HIGH STREET: original in **Dark Mind, Dark Heart**, ed. August Derleth (Arkham House: Sauk City, 1962, pp 249, $4.00); (Mayflower: London, 1963, wpps 222, ³⁄₆).

COLD PRINT: included in **Tales of the Cthulhu Mythos**, ed. August Derleth (q. v.).

THE INHABITANT OF THE LAKE AND LESS WELCOME TENANTS: Arkham House: Sauk City, 1964, pp 192, $4.00. Contents: *The Room in the Castle/The Horror from the Bridge/The Insects from Shaggai/The Render of the Veils/The Inhabitant of the Lake/The Plain of Sound/The Return of the Witch/The Mine on Yuggoth/The Moon-Lens*; plus *The Will of Stanley Brooke*, which is non-Mythos.

THE MINE ON YUGGOTH: included in **The Inhabitant of the Lake** (Arkham House: Sauk City, 1964, pp 192, $4.00—*see above*).

THE STONE ON THE ISLAND: original in **Over the Edge**, ed. August Derleth (Arkham House: Sauk City, 1964, pp vi + 297, $5.00).

LIN CARTER, ed.

THE SPAWN OF CTHULHU: Ballantine: N. Y., 02394, 1971, wpps 274, 95¢. Contents: *Introduction*, by Lin Carter/*The Whisperer in Darkness*, by H. P. Lovecraft/*An Inhabitant of Carcosa*, by Ambrose Bierce/*The Yellow Sign*, by Robert W. Chambers/*Cordelia's Song*, (verse) by Vincent Starrett/*The Return of Hastur*, by August Derleth/*Litany to Hastur*, (verse) by Lin Carter/*The Children of the Night*, by Robert E. Howard/*K'n-yan*, by Walter C. DeBill, Jr./*The Tale of Satampra Zeiros*, by Clark Ashton Smith/*The Hounds of Tindalos*, by Frank Belknap Long/*The Curse of Yig*, by Zealia Brown Reed Bishop/*The Mine on Yuggoth*, by J. Ramsey Campbell. Carter uses a somewhat loose definition of the Mythos.

HUGH B. CAVE

DEAD MAN'S BELT: *Weird Tales*, May 1933.

DEATH-WATCH: *Weird Tales*, June-July 1939.

ROBERT W. CHAMBERS

THE YELLOW SIGN: *Magazine of Horror* #1, October 1963; included in **Sleep No More**, ed. August Derleth (Rinehart: N. Y., 1944, pp 374, $2.50); (Armed Services edition, nd, np); included in **Masters of Horror**, ed. Alden H. Norton (Berkeley: N. Y., X1497, 1968, wpps 192, 60¢); included in **Horror Omnibus**, ed. Kurt Singer (W. H. Allen: London, 1965, pp 317, 25s); (Panther: London 2158, 1966, wpps 283, 5s); included in **The Spawn of Cthulhu**, ed. Lin Carter (q. v.); and of course in **The King in Yellow**.

AUGUST DERLETH

BEYOND THE THRESHOLD: *Weird Tales*, September 1941; included in **Tales of the Cthulhu Mythos**, ed. August Derleth (q. v.); in **Something Near** (Arkham House: Sauk City, 1945, pp 274, $3.00).

THE BLACK ISLAND: *Weird Tales*, January 1952; in **The Trail of Cthulhu** (Arkham House: Sauk City, 1962, pp 248, $4.00); (Beagle: N. Y., 95108, 1971, wpps 168, 95¢).

THE DWELLER IN DARKNESS: *Weird Tales*, November 1944; included in **Tales of the Cthulhu Mythos**, (q. v.); in **Something Near** (Arkham House: Sauk City, 1945, pp 274, $3.00).

THE HOUSE IN THE VALLEY: *Weird Tales*, July 1953; included in **Tales of Terror**, ed. Kurt Singer (W. H. Allen: London, 1967, pp 255, 30s); in **The Mask of Cthulhu** (Arkham House: Sauk City, 1958, pp 201, $3.50); (Beagle: N. Y., 95107, 1971, wpps 180, 95¢).

ITHAQUA: *Strange Stories*, February 1941; in **Something Near** (Arkham House: Sauk City, 1945, pp 274, $3.00).

THE KEEPER OF THE KEY: *Weird Tales*, May 1951; included in **Weird Tales of the Supernatural**, ed. Kurt Singer (W. H. Allen: London, 1966, pp 352, 30s); in **The Trail of Cthulhu** (Arkham House: Sauk City, 1962, pp 248, $4.00); (Beagle: N. Y., 95108, 1971, wpps 168, 95¢).

THE RETURN OF HASTUR: *Weird Tales*, March 1939; included in **The Spawn of Cthulhu**, ed. Lin Carter (q. v.); in **Someone in the Dark** (Arkham House: Sauk City, 1941, pp 335, $2.00); in **The Mask of Cthulhu** (Arkham House: Sauk City, 1958, pp 201, $3.50); (Beagle: N. Y., 95107, 1971, wpps 180, 95¢).

THE SANDWIN COMPACT: *Weird Tales*, November 1940; in **Someone in the Dark** (Arkham House: Sauk City, 1941, pp 335, $2.00); in **The Mask of Cthulhu** (Arkham House: Sauk City, 1958, pp 201, $3.50); (Beagle: N. Y., 95107, 1971, wpps 180, 95¢).

THE SEAL OF R'LYEH: *Fantastic Universe*, July 1957; in **The Mask of Cthulhu** (Arkham House: Sauk City, 1958, pp 201, $3.50); (Beagle: N. Y., 95107, 1971, wpps 180, 95¢).

SOMETHING FROM OUT THERE: *Weird Tales*, January 1951; in **The Mask of Cthulhu** (Arkham House: Sauk City, 1958, pp 201, $3.50); (Beagle: N. Y., 95107, 1971, wpps 180, 95¢).

SOMETHING IN WOOD: *Weird Tales*, March 1948; in **The Mask of Cthulhu** (Arkham House: Sauk City, 1958, pp 201, $3.50); (Beagle: N. Y., 95107, 1971, wpps 180, 95¢).

THE TESTAMENT OF CLAIBORNE BOYD: *Weird Tales*, March 1949; in **The Trail of Cthulhu** (Arkham House: Sauk City, 1962, pp 248, $4.00); (Beagle: N. Y., 95108, 1971, wpps 168, 95¢).

THE THING THAT WALKED ON THE WIND: *Strange Tales*, January 1933; included in **The Boris Karloff Horror Anthology** (Souvenir Press: London, 1965, pp 190, 21s); (Corgi: London GN7621, 1967, wpps 158, 3/6); (as **Boris Karloff's Favorite Horror Stories**: Avon: N. Y. G1254, 1965, wpps 176, 50¢); in **Something Near** (Arkham House: Sauk City, 1945, pp 274, $3.00).

THE TRAIL OF CTHULHU: *Weird Tales*, March 1944; in **The Trail of Cthulhu** (Arkham House: Sauk City, 1962, pp 248, $4.00); (Beagle: N. Y., 95108, 1971, wpps 168, 95¢).

THE WATCHER FROM THE SKY: *Weird Tales*, July 1945, in **The Trail of Cthulhu** (Arkham House: Sauk City, 1962, pp 248, $4.00); (Beagle: N. Y., 95108, 1971, wpps 168, 95¢).

THE WHIPPORWHILLS IN THE HILLS: *Weird Tales*, September 1948; in **The Mask of Cthulhu** (Arkham House: Sauk City, 1958, pp 201, $3.50); (Beagle: N. Y., 95107, 1971, wpps 180, 95¢).

AUGUST DERLETH and HPL

see the stories: *The Ancestor/The Dark Brotherhood/The Fisherman of Falcon Point/The Horror from the Middle Span/The Lurker at the Threshold/The Murky Glass/The Peabody Heritage/The Shadow in the Attic/The Shadow Out of Space/The Shuttered Room/The Survivor/Witches' Hollow.*

AUGUST DERLETH and MARK SCHORER

THE EVIL ONES: *Strange Stories*, October 1940; in **Colonel Markesan and Less Pleasant People** (Arkham House: Sauk City, 1966, pp 285, $5.00).

THE LAIR OF THE STAR-SPAWN: *Weird Tales*, August 1932; *Magazine of Horror* #14, Winter 1966; in **Colonel Markesan and Less Pleasant People** (Arkham House: Sauk City, 1966, pp 285, $5.00).

THE OCCUPANT OF THE CRYPT: *Weird Tales*, September 1947.

HENRY HASSE

THE GUARDIAN OF THE BOOK: *Weird Tales*, March 1937.

HAZEL HEALD

THE HORROR IN THE MUSEUM: *Weird Tales*, July 1933; included in **Dr. Caligari's Black Book**, ed. Peter Haining (W. H. Allen: London, 1968, pp 190, 21s); included in **Terror By Night**, ed. Christine Campbell Thomson (Selwyn Blount: London, 1934, pp 252, 2s); included in **Not At Night Omnibus**, ed. Christine Campbell Thomson (Selwyn Blount: London, 1937, pp 510, ⅖); included in **The Pan Book of Horror Stories**, ed. Herbert Van Thal (Pan: London X45, 1959, wpps 317, ⅜); (Gold Medal: N. Y., D1693, 1966, wpps 254, 50¢); in **Beyond the Wall of Sleep** (q. v.); in **The Horror in the Museum** (q. v.).

OUT OF THE EONS: *Weird Tales*, April 1933; included in **The Sleeping and the Dead**, ed. August Derleth (Pellegrini & Cudahy: N. Y., 1947, pp 518, $3.75); in **Beyond the Wall of Sleep** (q. v.); in **The Horror in the Museum** (q. v.).

ROBERT E. HOWARD

ARKHAM (verse): *Weird Tales*, August 1932; included in **Dark of the Moon**, ed. August Derleth (Arkham House: Sauk City, 1947, pp xvi + 318, $3.00); in **Always Comes Evening** (Arkham House: Sauk City, 1957, pp x + 86, $3.00).

THE BLACK STONE: *Weird Tales*, November 1931; *Weird Tales*, November 1953; included in **Grim Death**, ed. Christine Campbell Thomson (Selwyn Blount: London, 1932, pp 254, 2s); included in **Sleep No More**, ed. August Derleth (Rinehart: N. Y., 1944, pp 374, $2.50); (Armed Services edition nd, np); included in **Tales of the Cthulhu Mythos**, ed. August Derleth (q. v.); in **Skullface and Others**, Arkham House: Sauk City, 1946, pp x + 475, $5.00); in **Wolfshead** (Lancer: N. Y., 1968, wpps 190, 60¢).

CHILDREN OF THE NIGHT: *Weird Tales*, April-May 1931; included in **The Spawn of Cthulhu**, ed. Lin Carter (q. v.); in **The Dark Man and Others** (Arkham House: Sauk City, 1963, pp 284, $4.00); (Lancer: N. Y., 75265, 1972, wpps 254, 95¢).

DIG ME NO GRAVE: *Weird Tales*, February 1937; in **The Dark Man and Others** (Arkham House: Sauk City, 1963, pp 284, $4.00); (Lancer: N. Y., 75265, 1972, wpps 254, 95¢).

THE SHADOW KINGDOM: *Weird Tales*, August 1929; in **Skullface and Others**, (Arkham House: Sauk City, 1946, pp x + 475, $5.00); in **The Coming of Conan** (Gnome Press: N. Y., 1953, pp 224, $3.00); in **King Kull** (Lancer Books: N. Y., 1967, wpps 223, 60¢). Done in comic form in **Kull the Conqueror** #2 (1971).

THE THING ON THE ROOF: *Weird Tales*, February 1932; in **The Dark Man and Others** (Arkham House: Sauk City, 1963, pp 284, $4.00); (Lancer: N. Y., 75265, 1972, wpps 254, 95¢).

HENRY KUTTNER

BELLS OF HORROR (as by Keith Hammond): *Strange Stories*, April 1939.

THE FROG: *Strange Stories*, February 1939.

THE HUNT: *Strange Stories*, June 1939.

HYDRA: *Weird Tales*, April 1939.

THE INVADERS (as by Keith Hammond): *Strange Stories*, February 1939.

IT WALKS BY NIGHT: *Weird Tales*, December 1936.

THE SALEM HORROR: *Weird Tales*, May 1937; included in **Tales of the Cthulhu Mythos**, ed. August Derleth (q. v.).

THE SECRET OF KRALITZ: *Weird Tales*, October 1936.

THE WATCHER AT THE DOOR: *Weird Tales*, May 1939.

FRANK BELKNAP LONG

THE ABOMINABLE SNOWMEN (verse): *Weird Tales*, June-July 1931; included in **Dark of the Moon**, ed. August Derleth (Arkham House: Sauk City, 1947, pp xvi + 318, $3.00).

THE BRAIN EATERS: *Weird Tales*, June 1932; *Magazine of Horror* #21, May 1968.

THE HORROR FROM THE HILLS: *Weird Tales*, January and February-March 1931 (serial); Arkham House: Sauk City, 1963, pp 110, $3.00; as **Odd Science Fiction**, with two irrelevant short stories: Belmont: N. Y., 1965, wpps 160, 50¢.

THE HOUNDS OF TINDALOS: *Weird Tales*, March 1929; *Weird Tales*, July 1937; *Avon Fantasy Reader* #16, 1951; included in *Tales of the Cthulhu Mythos*, ed. August Derleth (q. v.); included in **The Spawn of Cthulhu**, ed. Lin Carter (q. v.); in **The Hounds of Tindalos** (Arkham House: Sauk City, 1946, pp 316, $3.00); (Belmont: N. Y., L92-569, 1963, wpps 173, 50¢).

THE MALIGNANT INVADER: *Weird Tales*, January 1932.

ON ICY KINARTH (verse): *Weird Tales*, April 1930.

THE SPACE EATERS: *Weird Tales*, July 1928; *Magazine of Horror* #1, November 1963; included in **Tales of the Cthulhu Mythos**, ed. August Derleth (q. v.); in **The Hounds of Tindalos** (Arkham House: Sauk City, 1946, pp 316, $3.00); (Belmont: N. Y., L92-569, 1963, wpps 173, 50¢).

WHEN CHAUGNAR WAKES (verse): *Weird Tales*, September, 1932.

BRIAN LUMLEY

CEMENT SURROUNDINGS: original in **Tales of the Cthulhu Mythos**, ed. August Derleth (q. v.).

THE SISTER CITY: original in **Tales of the Cthulhu Mythos**, ed. August Derleth (q. v.).

WILLIAM LUMLEY

THE DIARY OF ALONSO TYPER: *Weird Tales*, February 1938; in **Beyond the Wall of Sleep** (q. v.); in **Tales of the Cthulhu Mythos**, ed. August Derleth (q. v.).

ARTHUR MACHEN

THE NOVEL OF THE BLACK SEAL: included in **Tales to be Told in the Dark**, ed. Basil Davenport Dodd, Mead: N. Y., 1953, pp 335, $3.00); (Dodd: Toronto, $3.50); (Faber: London, 1953, pp 288, 15s); in **The Three Imposters** (various editions).

THE WHITE PEOPLE: included in **Tales to be Told in the Dark**, ed. Basil Davenport (Dodd, Mead: N. Y., 1953, pp 335, $3.00); (Dodd: Toronto, $3.50); (Faber: London, 1953, pp 288, 15s); included in **The Haunted Omnibus**, ed. Alexander Laing (Farrar & Rinehart: N. Y., 1937, pp 848,

$3.00); (Oxford: Toronto); (Cassell: London, 1937); (Garden City Publishing Co: N. Y., 1939, $1.79); (as **Great Ghost Stories of the World**: Blue Ribbon: N. Y., 1941, pp viii + 489, $1.00); (Blue Ribbon: Tor., $1.39); and various collections.

DUANE W. RIMEL

DREAMS OF YITH (verse): originally in an unknown fanzine in about 1940; included in **Dark of the Moon**, ed. August Derleth (Arkham House: Sauk City, 1947, pp xvi + 418, $3.00).

A Rimel story in the Mythos also appeared in a fanzine around 1940. No further information on it is currently available.

W. VERNON SHEA

THE HAUNTER OF THE GRAVEYARD: original in **Tales of the Cthulhu Mythos**, ed. August Derleth (q. v.).

CLARK ASHTON SMITH

THE COMING OF THE WHITE WORM: *Stirring Science Stories*, April 1941; in **Lost Worlds** (Arkham House: Sauk City, 1944, pp 419, $3.00); in **Hyperborea** (Ballantine: N. Y., 02206, 1971, wpps 205, 95¢).

THE DOOR TO SATURN: *Strange Tales*, January 1932; *Magazine of Horror* #6, November 1964; in **Lost Worlds** (Arkham House: Sauk City, 1944, pp 419, $3.00); in **Hyperborea** (Ballantine: N. Y., 02206, 1971, wpps 205, 95¢).

THE HOLINESS OF AZÉDARAC: *Weird Tales*, November 1933; *Magazine of Horror* #35, Winter 1971; in **Lost Worlds** (Arkham House: Sauk City, 1944, pp 419, $3.00).

THE NAMELESS OFFSPRING: *Strange Tales*, June 1932; *Magazine of Horror* #33, Summer 1970; in **The Abominations of Yondo** (Arkham House: Sauk City, 1960, pp 227, $4.00).

THE RETURN OF THE SORCEROR: *Strange Tales*, September 1931; *Startling Mystery Stories* #8, Spring 1968; included in **Sleep No More**, ed. August Derleth (Rinehart: N. Y., 1944, pp 374, $2.50); (Armed Services edition, nd, np); included in **Tales of the Cthulhu Mythos**, ed. August Derleth (q. v.); in **Out of Space and Time** (Arkham House: Sauk City, 1942, pp xii + 370, $3.00).

THE SEVEN GEASES: *Weird Tales*, October 1934; in **Lost Worlds** (Arkham House: Sauk City, 1944, pp 419, $3.00); in **Hyperborea** (Ballantine: N. Y., 02206, 1971, wpps 205, 95¢).

THE TALE OF SATAMPRA ZEIROS: *Weird Tales*, November 1931; included in **The Spawn of Cthulhu**, ed. Lin Carter (q. v.); in **Lost Worlds** (Arkham House: Sauk City, 1944, pp 419, $3.00); in **Hyperborea** (Ballantine: N. Y., 02206, 1971, wpps 205, 95¢).

THE TESTAMENT OF ATHAMMAUS: *Weird Tales*, October 1932; included in **Swords and Sorcery**, ed. L. Sprague deCamp (Pyramid: N. Y., #R-950, 1963, wpps 186, 50¢); in **Out of Space and Time** (Arkham House: Sauk City, 1942, pp xii + 370, $3.00); in **Hyperborea** (Ballantine: N. Y., 02206, 1971 wpps 205, 95¢).

UBBO-SATHLA: *Weird Tales*, July 1933; *Avon Fantasy Reader* #15, 1951; included in **The Second Avon Fantasy Reader**, ed. George Ernsberger and Donald A. Wollheim (Avon: N. Y., 5385, 1969, wpps 173, 60¢); included in **Tales of the Cthulhu Mythos**, ed. August Derleth (q. v.); in **Out of Space and Time** (Arkham House: Sauk City, 1942, pp xii + 370, $3.00); in **Hyperborea** (Ballantine: N. Y., 02206, 1971, wpps 205, 95¢).

THE WEIRD OF AVOOSL WUTHOQQUAN: *Weird Tales*, June 1932; included in **And the Darkness Falls**, ed. Boris Karloff (World: N. Y., 1946, pp 631, $2.75); included in **In Memoriam: Clark Ashton Smith**, ed. Jack L. Chalker (Anthem: Baltimore, 1963, wpps xiv + 98, $3.00; hardcover $7.50); in **Out of Space and Time** (Arkham House: Sauk City, 1942, pp xii + 370, $3.00); in **Hyperborea** (Ballantine: N. Y., 02206, 1971, wpps 205, 95¢).

C. HALL THOMPSON

SPAWN OF THE GREEN ABYSS: *Weird Tales*, November 1946.

THE WILL OF CLAUDE ASHUR: *Weird Tales*, July 1947.

JAMES WADE

THE DEEP ONES: original in **Tales of the Cthulhu Mythos**, ed. August Derleth (q. v.).

DONALD WANDREI

THE LADY IN GREY: *Weird Tales*, December 1933; in **The Eye and the Finger** (Arkham House: Sauk City, 1944, pp xiii + 344, $3.00).

SONNETS OF THE MIDNIGHT HOURS: collected in **Dark of the Moon**, ed. August Derleth (Arkham House: Sauk City, 1947, pp xvi + 418, $3.00); expanded in **Poems for Midnight** (Arkham House: Sauk City, 1964, pp 68, $3.75).

THE TREE-MEN OF M'BWA: *Weird Tales*, December 1933; in **The Eye and the Finger** (Arkham House: Sauk City, 1944, pp xiii + 344, $3.00).

MANLY WADE WELLMAN

THE TERRIBLE PARCHMENT: *Weird Tales*, August 1937.

COLIN WILSON

THE PHILOSOPHER'S STONE: Arthur Barker: London, 1971, pp   ,   ; Crown: N. Y., 1971, pp

THE RETURN OF THE LLOIGOR: original in **Tales of the Cthulhu Mythos**, ed. August Derleth (q. v.).

CHAPTER 7

Comics

CHAMBER OF DARKNESS

THE MUSIC OF ERICH ZANN: *Chamber of Darkness* #5, June 1970, *as* "The Music from Beyond." Art by Johnny Craig and script by Roy Thomas.

CREEPY

THE RATS IN THE WALLS: *Creepy* #21, July 1968. Art by Bob Jenney.

EERIE

WENTWORTH'S DAY: originally printed in **Treasury of Terror**, ed. Christopher Lee (Pyramid Books: N. Y., R-1498, 1966, wpps , ¢); *Eerie* #13, February 1968. Art and script by Russ Jones.

JOURNEY INTO MYSTERY

THE HAUNTER OF THE DARK: *Journey Into Mystery* #4, April 1973. Art by Gene Colan (pencils) and Dan Adkins (inks); script by Ron Goulart.

SKULL COMICS

COOL AIR: *Skull Comics* #4, 1972. By MCS.
THE HOUND: *Skull Comics* #4, 1972. By Jaxon.
PICKMAN'S MODEL: *Skull Comics* #4, 1972. By Arnold.
THE RATS IN THE WALLS: *Skull Comics* #5, 1972. By Corben.
THE SHADOW FROM THE ABYSS: *Skull Comics* #5, 1972. (Uncredited).
TO A DREAMER: *Skull Comics* #5, 1972. By C. Dalles.

TOWER OF SHADOWS

PICKMAN'S MODEL: *Tower of Shadows* #9, January 1971. Art by Tom Palmer and script by Roy Thomas.
THE TERRIBLE OLD MAN: *Tower of Shadows* #3, January 1970. Art by Barry Smith (inks by John Verpoorten and Dan Adkins); script by Roy Thomas.

VAULT OF HORROR

COOL AIR: *Vault of Horror* #17, February-March 1951,,*as* "Baby It's Cold Inside." Art by Ingels; script probably by Al Feldstein.

IN THE VAULT: *Vault of Horror* #16, December 1950-January 1951, *as* "Fitting Punishment." Art by Ingels; script probably by Al Feldstein.

NOTE: Credits are not given in the *Vault of Horror* stories, and this author speculates that these are possibly unauthorized adaptations of the HPL originals, based on a great similarity to the HPL stories. In addition there are probably many other unauthorized adaptations.

NOTE: Information on Comic Book adaptations of HPL stories arrived too late for cross-referencing in other chapters.

CHAPTER 8

On Lovecraft

THE PRODUCTION of material on Lovecraft is a *small* industry, never approaching the Chaucer or Melville factories in size, though at times almost matching them in triviality. The items included in Arkham House books (see under Collections) are almost all the material worth reading. However, there are a few other works worth reading, as follows:

ELDRITCH YANKEE GENTLEMAN: *by* L. Sprague de Camp, *Fantastic*, August and October, 1971, is well worth the trouble in locating, and augers well for his forthcoming biography of Lovecraft (from Doubleday).

H. P. L.: ed. and published by Meade and Penny Frierson (P. O. Box 9032, Crestline Hts., Birmingham, Alabama 35213), wpps 144, $3.00). This booklet dows not really contain any major articles, but should nevertheless be obtained by any means available, since the total effect of articles, fiction, and especially artwork, is unworldly.

H. P. L.: A MEMOIR: *by* August Derleth (Ben Abramson: N. Y., 1945, pp 122, $2.50), is worthwhile.

(H. P. L. issue): *Fresco*, Spring 1958.

LOVECRAFT: A LOOK BEHIND THE "CTHULHU MYTHOS": *by* Lin Carter (Ballantine: N. Y., 02427, 1972, wpps 198, 95¢), is mainly concerned with the development of the mythos, but also provides much information on Lovecraft's life, and is probably the best introduction to Lovecraftian studies we have yet had.

PORTRAIT IN WORDS: *by* James Warren Thomas, *Fresco*, Fall 1958 through Summer 1959, is an interesting attempt at a spiritual biography of Lovecraft.

Fifteen hundred copies, approximately, of this book have been printed and bound by Malloy Lithographing Inc., Ann Arbor, Michigan. The book is published for and distributed by The Mirage Press Ltd., a Baltimore, Maryland corporation, owned and operated by Jack L. Chalker, editorial director and sales manager and William E. Osten, production manager and book designer. The paper is an archival quality, acid-neutralized stock that should last for decades of normal use. The type was set in Century Schoolbook and Bodoni Book faces on a Varityper direct impression composing machine.